THE
LITTLE
GROWER'S
COOKBOOK

To our wonderful families: Nick, Arabella and Olivia;
Andrew, Will, Mima and George. You are our inspiration
for this book and our biggest supporters. We couldn't
have done it without you!

Lettuce Publishing

First published in 2021 by Lettuce Publishing UK and Singapore
Lettuce Publishing Limited
71-75 Shelton Street
Covent Garden
London WC2H 9JQ

www.lettucepublishing.com
info@lettucepublishing.com

Cover design: Mark Coltart
Illustrations and layout: Fiona Ritson and Mark Coltart
Photography: Ali Allen
Other photography: Julia Parker and Ghillie James as well
as Beton Studio, Slogger, Ruta Saulyte and Murdom6 at
dreamstime.com
Editor: Gemma Bowes

A CIP entry for this title is available from the British Library

ISBN 978-1-9163739-1-4

Colour reproduction by TWP Sdn Bhd

Publisher's Note:
Any child in a kitchen or garden should be supervised by a
parent or guardian at all times. Whilst every care has been taken
in compiling the recipes and activities in this book, Lettuce
Publishing, or any other persons who have been involved in
working on this publication, cannot accept responsibility for
any errors or omissions that may be found in the recipes or text,
nor for any problems or injuries that may arise as a result of
following a recipe or carrying out an activity in this book.

THE
LITTLE
GROWER'S
COOKBOOK

COOKING + GROWING + ACTIVITIES
PROJECTS FOR EVERY SEASON

Ghillie James & Julia Parker

Julia Parker is the author of a monthly online article *Veg on the Ledge* for LEON and runs popular fruit and veg growing courses from her home in Sussex. Julia's growing projects, using only sustainable and recycled products, are being showcased with Alitex at the Chelsea Flower Show.

Ghillie James is the author of four books including *Jam, Jelly and Relish* and *Grains are Good*. She was the food editor at Sainsbury's Magazine and now writes for a variety of publications including The Boston Globe, BBC Good Food Magazine and The Straits Times, Singapore.

This dynamic team first worked together on the Tesco Food Magazine and have relished teaming up again to write *The Little Grower's Cookbook* to share their love of kids, nature, gardening and healthy eating.

To find out more about Lettuce Publishing please visit www.lettucepublishing.com

You can also follow Lettuce Publishing on instagram @lettucepublishing

FOREWORD

By Olivia Colman

Some of the most treasured and clearest memories that I have from my childhood days in Norfolk are those that were spent outside in the fresh air. I remember that we used to pick samphire, cook it on a camping stove and dip it in butter. Simple pleasures but joyful ones. Our three children are at their happiest too, when given free rein to get outside in the fresh air and just be kids!

This connection to nature is more important now than ever before. Children are expected to grow up so fast, in these social media, gadget-dominated, crazy times. The book that Julia and Ghillie have written has resonated with me, as it is a wonderful reminder of the pure joy that children find in and with nature. It offers simple and sustainable gardening projects, recipes and weekend activities that anyone, anywhere can do, even in small urban spaces. Children will love choosing activities to try through the seasons.

The benefits of getting children outside into the fresh air and away from the all-pervading screens have consistently been proven. This lovely book is a great way to start.

Look out for:

 Easy-peasy activities

 Rainy day activities

Chapter One: Gardening Basics

What plants need and useful tools 10
Types of soil 13
Let's recycle 14
10 ways to save the planet 16
Welcome wildlife! 18
Seasonal planting and harvesting chart 20

Chapter Two: Get Planting!

Spring – carrots and parsnips, herbs, leeks, tomatoes and potatoes 22
Summer – lettuce, squashes and pumpkins, peas and strawberries 42
Autumn – beetroot and radishes, pea shoots, onions and greens 60
Winter – cress, garlic and blueberries 78

Chapter Three: Get Cooking!

Onions, root veggies, potatoes and garlic 94
Salad leaves, herbs and edible flowers 116
Broccoli, pak choi and all things green 130
Pumpkins, courgettes, cucumbers and tomatoes 142
Orchard fruits, summer berries and rhubarb 156

Chapter Four: Weekend Fun!

Little pots of sunshine – plant some flower seeds in homemade pots 180
Feed the birds – make your own seed feeders 182
Magical flower potions – create your own flower-scented water 184
Plant your packed lunch! – make a mini greenhouse 186
A café for worms – design your very own wormery 188
A present from the garden – herb-filled jam jars for someone special 190
Host a butterfly banquet – feed your fluttery friends their favourite foods 192
Build a bug hotel – construct a mini beast mansion 194
Store your seeds from A-Z – design your own seed library 196

GARDENI

NG BASICS

GARDENING BASICS

What plants need

Plants are living organisms and need four things to grow big and strong: water, sunlight, air and food, just like us. The sunshine helps the plants make their own energy to grow. This is called photosynthesis. Soil contains the food that plants need to grow – nitrogen, potassium and phosphorous. It also holds roots in place to stop plants from falling over. Water carries the food from the soil up through the roots, into the stem and to the leaves.

FIVE USEFUL TOOLS YOU WILL NEED

These basic tools will help you to become a Little Grower. They can be bought in smaller sizes to fit smaller hands.

1. **Garden fork**
   Mainly used for weeding, turning over soil and lifting out veggies like potatoes without slicing them in half.
2. **Garden spade**
   For digging, adding compost and moving plants from one place to another.
3. **Trowel**
   This is a smaller hand-held spade, useful for digging in little spaces and making holes in the soil/compost. Trowels can also be used for weeding.
4. **Secateurs**
   There is always some picking, tidying or stem cutting to be done. Secateurs are like a very sharp pair of scissors.
5. **Watering can/spray bottle**
   A must for every little grower, plants need water to grow. You can use a rinsed out empty cleaning spray bottle, filled with water, for spraying seeds and soil. You can also make your own watering can, see page 15.

HOW TO MAKE COMPOST

It's easy even if you don't have a garden. Just follow these steps:

1. Find a bucket or old dustbin with a lid, preferably made from plastic to keep the compost warm. This speeds up the process.
2. Ask an adult to make holes in the bottom of your container using a screwdriver or drill and put it somewhere on the ground outside.
3. Start adding your green and brown waste (see homegrown compost on the right) and cover with a lid.
4. Keep topping it up with more waste as it rots. It will produce a liquid which will drain away through the holes in the bottom; these same holes will let friendly bugs in.
5. To speed up the rotting process, mix the compost with a garden fork whenever you add more waste. This adds air which helps everything break down faster.

Types of soil

GARDEN SOIL

There are three main types of soil – clay, sandy and loamy. The best way to tell what type you have is to squeeze a bit into a ball. Clay soil will be thick and sticky, sandy will be fine, and loamy is smooth and light. Soil found in the garden can lack the things that plants need to grow big and strong. Mixing in compost (see below) will add nutrients to help plants grow well.

HOMEMADE COMPOST

Making your own compost is a great way to make sure plants get the food they need to help them grow, it's also a good way to recycle household waste (see left). Compost is a mix of green and brown waste. Green waste is old plants, vegetable peelings, old soil, grass or dead flowers. Brown waste is brown paper, egg boxes, wood chippings, cardboard, teabags, coffee grounds, wood ash and straw. Mixed together it all rots down over a long time to produce a dark crumbly soil. It is full of bugs and worms who break it down: their poo turns into plant food!

It will take 6–9 months before it turns into a lovely crumbly compost that you can then mix with soil to grow your fruit and veggies.

BOUGHT COMPOST/ MULTI-PURPOSE COMPOST OR POTTING COMPOST

This is different to homemade. It is a mix of soil and plant feed which is sold for growing seedlings and plants in containers as it helps plants grow stronger. This is the best type of compost to use for growing seeds and small plants, and for using for the projects in this book.

LEAF COMPOST

This is useful to use on top of the soil to help keep moisture in and stop the plants drying out. It is known as a mulch. To make it, you can reuse old compost bags or bin bags:

1. Make a few holes in the bottom of the bag and collect handfuls of autumn leaves when you are out and about. Pile them into the bag until it is nearly full.
2. Add some water on top and tie it shut.
3. Leave in a shady spot until the following autumn or longer. By then all the leaves will have rotted down to a damp mixture.
4. Sprinkle this on the top of the soil in your pots or veggie patch.

Little Grower's Tip

The important thing to remember when making your own compost is not to add cooked food, as this will encourage the wrong bugs and wildlife.

Let's recycle!

If you look around your home and outside there are probably lots of pots and containers that could happily double up as planters. This will help save the planet and your pocket money! Some containers that are not made from natural materials will need drainage holes made in the bottom with a screwdriver or skewer. Ask an adult to help you.

1. Card toilet roll tubes arranged on a tray make brilliant tall pots to sow seeds in.
2. Egg boxes and fruit punnets can be used as seed trays.
3. Yogurt pots, big or small, make brilliant pots for sowing.
4. Old ice cream containers, sweetie tins, dip pots, tin cans, plastic tubs, DIY trugs, old wellies, buckets, dustbins, car tyre rims and guttering are all suitable – be inventive!
5. Even reusable shopping bags are great containers for bigger plants to grow in.

MAKE YOUR OWN ECO-POTS

You can make biodegradeable plant pots using old newspaper and a tin can (see page 181).

You can also wash out empty egg shells, fill them with compost, plant a few seeds and when the seedlings are big enough, break the shell off around the roots and replant them into a bigger container.

Little Grower's Tip

Save broken egg shells and scatter pieces around the growing plant to stop slugs and snails from nibbling your seedlings.

Little Grower's Tip

The halved bases of plastic milk or juice bottles, cut at an angle, make great planters. You can use the handles to hang them from hooks as a space saver.

MAKE A WATERING CAN

Old plastic milk bottles or juice bottles with handles can be easily turned into watering cans. Wash them out, make 3–4 holes in the lid and fill with water, then try watering a plant. If the water comes out too slowly just make another hole or two.

DIY WATER SPRAYER

Rather than throwing away or recycling used plastic cleaning bottles – the ones with a spray nozzle – wash them out properly, with the help of an adult, and fill them with water. They are useful for watering tiny seeds when they are first sown as the spray mist is so fine the seeds are not dislodged or disturbed before they have a chance to grow.

10 ways to save the planet

1. **Grow your own** fruit and veggies at home and forage from the hedgerows, trees and bushes – both are fun and eco-friendly ways to get food. See our planting and harvesting guides on pages 20 and 21 to help you.

2. **Swap seedlings** and plants with friends.

3. **Buy seasonally** and locally to avoid products that are the result of unnecessary transportation. Visit local farmers' markets and independent shops that support local farmers and suppliers, and see what they are selling at different times of the year. Seasonal, organic and homegrown produce tastes better too!

4. **Make your own pots** using biodegradable materials. Recycle/repurpose other containers (see pages 14, 15 and 181) rather than buying new plastic ones.

5. **Save rain water** in a container or water butt and use it for watering your plants. To make your own nettle plant feed see 'Save The Planet Tip' on page 64.

6. **Make natural pesticides** rather than using chemical sprays to get rid of bugs or diseases, which might destroy your happy plants. You can use a squirt of washing up liquid, diluted with water, to spray the bugs on your plants.

7. **Collect seeds** from plants to re-use.

8. **Host a plant or bake sale** and raise money for your favourite planet-saving charity.

9. **Reduce waste** by using old containers as planters, saving wooden lolly sticks for plant markers, and making compost with green and brown household waste to use in the garden (see page 12). Look for plants sold with bare roots rather than in plastic pots to cut down on the use of plastic.

10. **Plant a tree** as a habitat for wildlife and to produce clean air; trees absorb carbon dioxide and make oxygen for us and other animals to breathe.

Welcome wildlife

Go wild. If you have some space, allow your garden to go wild in places. Let nettles, native wild flowers, weeds and grasses grow to attract wildlife such as bugs, birds, bees, caterpillars and butterflies (see page 192 for how to host a butterfly banquet). Wildflowers are a feeding ground, hiding and nesting place for birds, insects and small animals such as voles, frogs, newts and hedgehogs. Grasses are also a great hiding place for small animals and the seed heads are essential food. The numbers of these beautiful creatures are getting smaller every year so by giving them a safe and happy home you will help them survive.

Go online. Read books, or ask at your local garden centre, to learn which plants make good homes for the birds, bugs, bees and butterflies that live near to you. Have a look at some of the projects in this book's weekend activity pages, such as the bug hotel on page 195 to inspire you.

Feed the birds. Leave some of your flowers and plants to grow tall and go to seed in the autumn. Birds can feast on the seeds in the winter when there is not much else around for them to eat.

Bee kind. Grow bee-friendly plants. Bees love herbs, flowers, fruit and veggies as they collect pollen from the flowers which they can take back to their hives. We need bees to pollinate our plants. Get involved and support a local beekeeper. Buy local honey too as it has a great many health benefits.

Little Grower's Tip

Put up a bird box and hang the seed feeders from it (see page 182) to attract feathered friends. Leave a broken pot or two outside to provide shelter for hedgehogs.

WHEN TO SOW, PLANT AND HARVEST

Know which season you can sow your seeds, plant your seedlings, pick your fruit and veggies or buy the tastiest produce!

SPRING	
SOW OR PLANT	**HARVEST/BUY**
Beetroot	Asparagus
Carrots	Broccoli
Courgettes	Cress
Cress	Herbs
Garlic	Leeks
Herbs (plant)	Mango
Leeks	Pea shoots
Lettuce	Peas
Mangetout	Pineapple
Onions	Radishes
Parsnips	Rhubarb
Pea shoots	
Peas	
Potatoes	
Radishes	
Runner beans	
Strawberries (plant)	
Tomatoes	

SUMMER	
SOW OR PLANT	**HARVEST/BUY**
Beetroot	Apricots
Broccoli	Aubergine
Carrots	Beans
Courgettes (plant)	Beetroot
Cress	Blackberries
Herbs (plant)	Carrots
Kale	Cherries
Leeks	Courgettes
Lettuce	Cress
Mangetout	Garlic
Pak choi	Herbs
Pea shoots	Lettuce
Peas	Nectarines
Potatoes	Mango
Pumpkins (plant)	Melon
Radishes	Onions
Spinach and chard	Pea shoots
Strawberries (plant)	Peas and mangetout
	Peaches
	Peppers
	Plums
	Potatoes
	Radishes
	Rhubarb
	Summer berries
	Tomatoes

AUTUMN	
SOW OR PLANT	**HARVEST/BUY**
Beetroot	Apples
Broccoli	Beetroot
Carrots	Carrots
Cress	Cress
Herbs (plant)	Courgettes
Kale	Herbs
Lettuce	Leeks
Onions	Lettuce
Pak choi	Mangetout
Pea shoots	Pea shoots
Radishes	Pears
Spinach and chard	Potatoes
Strawberries (plant)	Pumpkins
	Radishes
	Raspberries

WINTER	
SOW OR PLANT	**HARVEST/BUY**
Blueberries	Beetroot
Broad beans	Brussels Sprouts
Cress	Cabbage
Garlic	Carrots
Pea shoots	Cauliflower
Radishes	Celery
Winter lettuce	Cranberries
	Cress
	Herbs
	Kale
	Leeks
	Parsnips
	Pea shoots
	Pears
	Pomegranate
	Radishes
	Spinach and chard
	Winter salads

Little Grower's Tip

As well as growing produce at home, look out for fruit and vegetables in season at your local farmers' market. You can use this chart to help you.

GET PLA

ANTING!
Spring

BUCKET & SPADE VEGGIES

Carrots and parsnips are much easier to grow in a bucket rather than in the ground, and any leftover sand in the bottom of your container will make the carrots even happier as they love fine, sandy soil!

There are lots of different varieties of carrots to choose from. Not all are orange – there are purple and white ones too. Some carrots are short and round like a table tennis ball! No matter what type you grow there is nothing better than homegrown carrots and parsnips, as they are deliciously sweet and packed full of vitamins. If you want to grow lots of veggies then use two buckets and two spades.

The basics

WHEN TO GROW

Spring is the perfect time to grow most parsnips and carrots, although some carrot varieties can be grown throughout the year.

YOU WILL NEED

- Large recycled seaside bucket (big enough for a full sized plant, you will need to add drainage holes)
- Recycled plastic spade
- Screwdriver or skewer to make holes in the bottom of the bucket
- Multi-purpose or potting compost
- Carrot and/or parsnip seeds
- Watering can
- Stick or pencil
- Waterproof coloured pens or paints

Preparation

BE SOIL READY

Carrots hate stony soil, while parsnips aren't so fussy. Stones can stop carrots from growing long, and instead turn them into strange alien shapes. So, make sure that you remove any stones or lumps from your compost before you fill the bucket. If you have any fine sand left over from an old sand pit or a visit to the beach then mix some of this in with the compost. Carrots love fine, sandy soil to help them grow big and straight. Ask an adult to help you make 4–5 drainage holes in the bottom of the bucket using a screwdriver or metal skewer.

Using a waterproof pen or paints, mark your spade paddle with a picture to remind you what is growing in each bucket. Once the bucket is half full of soil, bury the spade upside down with the handle in the soil and the paddle sticking out so that you can read it. Continue to fill the bucket to the brim, then give it a little shake or gently tap it on the ground to release any air pockets in the soil. Then water the soil to make it damp.

How to grow

SOWING

Seeds vary in size; carrot seeds are tiny and parsnip seeds are bigger. Carefully tip a few seeds into your hand. Make a few holes in the soil, each one 2cm deep and spaced 5cm apart, using a stick or a pencil. Spacing them equally apart allows the plants room to grow.

Drop either 3 carrot seeds or 1 parsnip seed into each hole and cover gently with some compost. The 3 seeds won't all grow into carrots, as not all the seeds will germinate (begin to grow) so sowing more than one gives safety in numbers. Seal the seed packets back up to sow more later on in the year (this is called successional sowing – see our seed library on page 196).

Using a watering can with a fine sprinkle (called a rose head), lightly water the top of the compost, being careful not to over water. Carrots and parsnips like a lot of sunshine so find a sunny spot outside and position your bucket on a table or chair to keep it away from pests (see Little Grower's Tip above).

GROWING

It's important not to let the soil in your bucket dry out. It's useful to set a time to check the soil every day (after breakfast for example, so you don't forget) and if the soil feels dry give it a light water.

In about two weeks you will see pairs of tiny green leaves appear. These are seedlings. Choose the strongest seedling and carefully pull out the other two. This is called thinning out. Don't be tempted to replant these smaller seedlings as they will not grow properly. Parsnips won't need thinning out in the same way as carrots. If you don't thin out the seedlings when they are first growing you may have more small carrots than large ones.

HARVESTING

Soon you will start to see carrots growing under lots of feathery green leaves. Keep watering as the vegetables grow to ensure they don't dry out.

Carrots can be picked at any stage, and are usually ready for pulling 2 months after sowing the seeds. For bigger carrots, leave them in for longer.

Parsnips won't be ready to harvest until the winter. They will mature in about 16 weeks and will be ready to pull up once the leaves begin to die back.

Let's get cooking with carrots and parsnips!

Orange dip – page 100
Cheesy root veg bake – page 111
Gardener's cake – page 112

Little Grower's Tip

Parsnips are ready to dig up after it starts to turn colder. The cold turns the starches into sugar, which makes a sweeter parsnip.

SHOPPING FOR HERBS

This is a fun way to make use of a big, reusable cloth (hessian) shopping bag, as the fabric has natural holes. Thick plastic reusable shopping bags also work well, but with some holes made for drainage. Keep your bag near the door so you can help yourself to fresh herbs whenever you want. It is better to buy young 'plug' plants as seeds take a long time to grow. Herb plants are easy to find for little money and can be bought during any season – farm shops, local markets and garden centres all sell a good selection. Buy them small and they will grow better for you.

The basics

WHEN TO GROW

Herbs are just the best as they can be grown all year round, inside and out!

YOU WILL NEED

- Old or broken reusable shopping bag or even better, a hessian fabric one
- Small herb 'plug' plants eg mint, basil, coriander, thyme, parsley, sage, marjoram, chives, rosemary
- Multi-purpose compost or potting compost
- Metal skewer or scissors to make drainage holes
- Garden trowel
- Horticultural grit (fine stones)
- Watering can
- Labels (wooden lolly sticks) and a pen or pencil

Find out how to turn your home-grown herbs into tasty presents from the garden on page 191.

Save The Planet Tip

If you buy perennial herbs (plants that grow for many years) such as lavender, sage, rosemary and mint they can stay in the bag at the end of their growing season, ready to burst into action the following spring.

Little Grower's Tip

Perennial herbs need to be cut back (pruned) every spring to stop them getting too big. Ask an adult to help you. The old woody stems should be removed to encourage tender leaves to grow from the bottom of the herb plant.

Preparation

BE SOIL READY

Herbs are not fussy and will grow in multi-purpose or potting compost, homemade compost or grow bag soil (which you can buy from garden centres). Move your bag to a sunny place, maybe by the front or back door so you can easily harvest your herbs. It's best to move it before you add the compost because it will be heavy. Hessian bags won't need dranage holes but if you're using a reusable shopping bag, make some small holes in the bottom using a skewer or scissors. Fill your bag to just below the top, mixing in a handful of small stones to help with drainage.

How to grow

PLANTING

Once you have chosen your herbs (3–4 plants are probably enough for a medium size shopping bag) dig a hole slightly bigger than one of the herbs, water the hole and wait for the water to drain away. Carefully remove the little herb plant from its pot and place in the hole. Fill in some soil around the base and gently press the soil down firmly in place using your hands. Do this with each herb until you have planted them all. Pop in named lolly sticks to label them.

GROWING

Water your herbs once a week until the weather warms up, then during the summer water every day. Even if it rains you must still water them, because when the plants grow bigger the rain will just fall off the leaves, missing the compost completely. Herbs are thirsty plants. Keep picking the fresh leaves as this will help the plant to produce more. In early summer they will start to flower, pick these off and use them, as all herb flowers are edible too! See our Gardener's cake recipe on page 112.

HARVESTING

You can pick the leaves from spring until the autumn, remove any flowers when they appear with scissors or by snapping them off. Flowering stops leaf production so by cutting off the flowering stems, you'll get more tender leaves!

Let's get cooking with herbs!

The best pesto for kids – page 127
Rainbow rolls – page 124
Gardener's cake – page 112
Squiggly noodle soup – page 137

Little Grower's Tip

Mint grows very quickly and the roots can take over and strangle other plants. So, either plant mint in its own bag or with just one other annual herb, such as basil or coriander.

WE'VE SPRUNG A LEEK!

From the same 'allium' family as onions, leeks are sweeter and packed full of vitamins and fibre. They also make themselves useful to the other plants in the garden as their smell keeps pesky, veggie munching pests away! Leeks like to be mostly left alone and they don't need much space to grow. However, they do need watering regularly in the dry months.

The basics

WHEN TO GROW

Early spring is the perfect time to sow leek seeds inside, just as the weather starts to warm up. You can also choose to buy tiny seedling plants (plugs) instead, which can go straight into the bigger container outside.

The best way to sow leek seeds is inside, in a recycled, clear plastic fruit container – the kind you buy your strawberries in. You can just sow a few seeds to begin with, then sow some more every 3–4 weeks until the summer. This is called successional sowing (see page 196).

YOU WILL NEED

- Plastic clear fruit punnet or old yogurt pot
- Screwdriver or skewer for making drainage holes
- Tray
- Water sprayer (use an old cleaning spray bottle, once washed out)
- Packet of leek seeds or shop bought leek seedlings (plugs)
- Old deep plastic watering can, or bucket, the larger the better
- Multi-purpose or potting compost
- Stick or pencil
- Watering can

Little Grower's Tip

A plastic watering can is easier to make drainage holes in. If using a metal one, you will need an adult to drill some holes.

Save the Planet Tip

There are too many leek seeds in a packet to sow all at once. So when you have sown some, fold over the foil envelope and save the rest for another sowing later. See page 196 for how to label and decorate your envelopes.

Little Grower's Tip

Place your leeks near carrots, if you are growing them. The strong smell from leeks will help keep nasties such as carrot root fly away.

Preparation

CHOOSE YOUR CONTAINER

Find a clear plastic supermarket punnet or old yogurt pots. You will need to ask an adult to help you to make 2–3 holes in the bottom of the pots for drainage, using a screwdriver or skewer (an old punnet already has them). Your watering can or bucket will also need drainage holes, which you can make using a screwdriver or skewer (see the tip to the left).

SOWING

If you are planting leek seedlings (small plants, called 'plugs', rather than seeds) you can move straight to the transplanting section below.

Fill your punnet or pots with multi-purpose or potting compost, remove any larger lumps from the compost by rubbing the soil through your fingers, and sprinkle with a little water to make it damp.

Carefully sprinkle a few of the tiny black leek seeds on top of the damp compost. Now sprinkle a little more compost on top to protect them and water lightly again. The spray bottle is perfect for this. Place your pots on a tray to catch water spills and pop on a warm sunny window ledge to help speed up germination, or leave them outside in a sheltered sunny spot.

How to grow

GROWING

Leek seeds sown inside will take about 1 week to germinate. Outside will take a little longer.

TRANSPLANTING

When the the small leek plants are about 9 weeks old they should look like pencil thin shoots. You can now plant them in your watering can or bucket. Make sure your container has 4–5 drainage holes in the bottom. Fill it with multi-purpose compost to just below the top. Pick it up and tap it on the ground a few times to remove any air pockets. Using an old pencil, make lots of holes spaced about 8–10cm apart and 6cm deep. Carefully prize apart any seedlings stuck together and drop one, roots first, into each hole. Do this until you run out of seedlings or space. A large watering can or big bucket will have room for about 10 leeks. Then water them in using another watering can. Don't worry if your leeks fall over when you move them, they will quickly recover once watered.

As the leeks grow bigger, you can build the soil up at the base of each one, like a little mole hill or mound, this is called 'earthing up'. It blocks out the light on the growing stems so you end up with even longer white leek stems (the tasty part). You don't have to do this, but it can make them taste sweeter.

HARVESTING

Water your leeks regularly. The first leek should be ready in about 20 weeks, during the summer. You can harvest them small or big, it's up to you. Don't eat them all too soon because it is nice to be able to harvest them during the autumn and winter too. Just lift them carefully as and when you need them. They will happily grow outside all winter. Why not sow more seeds in the summer so you will have lots more leeks to eat in the winter too?

Let's get cooking with leeks!

Mini but mighty baked veggie bites – page 104

Little Grower's Tip

It's a good idea to mark on the calender when your leeks should be ready for pulling up, as it's quite a long wait!

Little Grower's Tip

Allow one leek to grow late into the summer. When it forms a stalk with a flower, that flower will turn into tiny seed heads (see right). When the heads are dry, tap or shake the seeds into a jam jar and store in an envelope with your other seeds (see seed library on page 196). Sow the dry seeds again next year.

A CAN OF TOMATOES

Tomatoes are actually a fruit not a vegetable. They are easy to grow from seed but you can also buy young plants from your local farmers' markets or garden centre. There are lots of varieties to choose from in different colours and sizes as well as two types – 'bush' tomatoes and taller 'cordon' tomato plants. Here we used the bush (also known as compact) tomato as it will grow happily in a large container (ask your local pizza restaurant for an extra large tomato or olive tin) and it will reward you with lots of tasty fruits. Homegrown tomatoes, picked stright from the plant, remind Julia of her childhood – harvesting sweet, juicy tomatoes, full of flavour and scent, with her father in his greenhouse.

The basics

WHEN TO GROW

Sow seeds in spring and plant in early summer, when the weather is warmer.

YOU WILL NEED

- Packet of bush (compact) tomato seeds or 1 small bush or compact tomato plant
- Recycled supermarket fruit punnet, small yogurt pots or biodegradable pots
- Bigger yogurt pots or drink cups for transplanting
- Tray
- Recycled, extra-large tin, about 20–25cm tall, clean and with no sharp edges or 1 large deep flower pot
- Multi-purpose or potting compost
- Growbag compost (this is a compost from a garden centre that is good for growing tomatoes)
- Plant label (wooden lolly stick), pen or pencil
- Watering can
- Stick for supporting the plant, such as a bamboo cane
- Gardener's twine or string

If you are using tomato plants rather than seeds then you can skip straight to the transplanting section.

SOWING

A recycled, clean fruit punnet, small yogurt pots or biodegrable pots are the perfect containers to grow your tomato plants from seed. Fill each punnet or pot with your compost, rubbing it through your hands to remove any lumps, and add some water. Sow one seed per cup or six seeds per punnet and top up with a little more compost. Alternatively, see our 'mini greenhouse' project on page 186 for a fun way to do this using a fresh tomato.

GROWING

About two weeks after sowing, your tomato seedlings will have appeared. When they are about 8cm tall and have two true leaves you will need to move them to the large yogurt pots or drinks cups to continue growing. You will need to make some drainage holes in the bottom.

Using a pencil, make a hole in the compost. The seedlings will have very thin stems so carefully pick them up by their leaves and place into the hole gently, one plant for each pot, trying not to damage the roots. Water the seedlings carefully and leave in a sunny warm place; tomatoes need lots of light to stop them becoming thin and weak. Don't forget to label your plants and stand the pots on a tray to catch water spills.

TRANSPLANTING

When your seedlings have 3–4 true leaves you can transplant them to the extra-large tin or large deep flowerpot that you have filled with grow bag compost. Tomatoes are hungry plants and will love the rich nutrients in this compost. Water the plants regularly but be careful not to overwater if your container does not have drainage holes. When the weather warms up, move them outside to a sunny, sheltered spot.

HARVESTING

Bush tomato plants need little attention other than watering daily. Soon lots of yellow flowers will appear and each one of these flowers will turn into a tomato. Your first tomatoes will be ripe and ready to pick by midsummer, but more tomatoes will keep coming! Keep checking your plants to see when the tomatoes start to turn red – that's when to pick them. If there are lots of sunny days the tomatoes will ripen very quickly.

Little Grower's Tip

Plant some basil near your tomato plants. The lovely scent from the leaves will stop white fly attacking your plants. Or even better try the 'pizza box' idea on the next page.

Little Grower's Tip

When transplanting your tomato plants, bury them deeply - including some of the stem into the compost - this helps increase the root system, making your plants big and strong.

FUN IDEA – GROW YOUR OWN PIZZA BOX!

If you have an old wooden crate, wine box or similar you can grow your favourite pizza ingredients in one place. Fill the box with grow bag compost and plant tomato, basil, oregano, chives, chillies and onions, or whatever you prefer, put in a warm sunny place and just remember to water them daily.

Let's get cooking with tomatoes!

Terrific tray bake pizza – page 146
Ten veg soup – page 140
Ketchup – page 150

Little Grower's Tip

Tomatoes are self-pollinating which means they don't need another tomato plant or bees to help produce fruit, unlike some other fruit and vegetables. You can give them a helping hand by gently shaking the plants when the yellow flowers appear; this spreads more pollen and guarantees lots of juicy tomatoes for you.

A SACK OF POTATOES

Potatoes are the easiest veggies to grow; they need very little attention, are fast growing and taste amazing! Potato plants will reward you with heaps of spuds, which appear out of the ground, rather like treasure, when you dig them up. One plant will produce about 15 potatoes. You don't need lots of space to grow them either – a sack makes an excellent container! William, Ghillie's eldest son, loves digging up potatoes with his Grandpa.

The basics

WHEN TO GROW

There are three different groups of potatoes to grow, all of which are usually planted in the spring. The three groups are: 'Earlies', which are first to crop in early summer; 'Second Earlies', which are ready in midsummer; and 'Maincrop' which are larger and take longer to mature so they are ready in late summer/early autumn and are stored to use over winter. Use two or three sacks if you fancy growing a few varieties.

YOU WILL NEED

- Seed potatoes (you can buy these from a garden centre, they look like any normal eating potato but are specially prepared to produce a crop that is disease resistant)
- Multi-purpose or homemade compost
- Spade
- Watering can
- Garden fork
- Hessian fabric sack or old compost bag. Once planted, each seed potato will turn into 10–15 new potatoes! So make sure your sack is big enough. Compost bags will need 4–5 holes made in the bottom for drainage.

Little Grower's Tip

To speed up the process, place seed potatoes upright in an empty eggbox. Make sure the eyes point upwards (the little black dots). Keep them in a light place, like a windowsill or table. Green shoots will soon appear and in about a month they will be ready to plant out. This is called 'chitting'.

Little Grower's Tip

Grow some mint nearby, that way you can pick both at the same time. Mint is the perfect herb to boil with potatoes.

Little Grower's Tip

Do not use a spade when harvesting as it can slice a potato in half as you dig it up. A fork is better.

Preparation

BE SOIL READY

Multi-purpose compost is ideal or homemade compost is even better. Pile your compost into the sack or bag until about halfway up. Add a little water.

How to grow

POSITION YOUR CONTAINER

Choose a sunny spot for your sack (make sure an adult knows you are going to use it for about 15–20 weeks, as the sack will be heavy and not so easy to move once planted). Check the weather forecast before starting, and make sure that no cold weather is forecast.

PLANTING

Place 3 seed potatoes on top of the compost in the sack allowing space between each one. Pile more compost carefully on top of these seed potatoes so as not to disturb their position; leave some room in the sack for more compost later. Water again carefully so you don't uncover the potatoes.

GROWING

Very soon you will start to see green leaves pushing through the soil. Add some more compost to cover these leaves, this gives them added protection from colder weather. This is called earthing up. Water your sack regularly in dry weather once you see the green leaves emerge. Soon enough, the leaves and stems will be growing so fast that it will be impossible to cover them with earth any more.

HARVESTING

Your potato plant will start to flower 12–15 weeks from planting. This means your potatoes are ready for harvesting. Carefully tip the sack onto its side and slide the compost out using a garden digging fork. You will see lots of potatoes attached to thin roots, just pull them off. Make sure you wash them before use.

Let's get cooking with potatoes!

Sausage and veggie sleepover – page 108
Cheesy root veg bake – page 111
Hedgehog potatoes – page 107

ANTING!
Summer

PICK 'N' MIX LETTUCE

Lettuce is easy to grow from seed and is packed full of goodness. There is nothing better than having your very own lettuce supply right outside your door, plastic and packaging free. The leaves don't have to be green and boring, there are lots of bright colours to choose from. Have you ever seen a purple or red lettuce?

Some lettuces are soft and buttery and some are crunchy, all with a slightly different flavour. If you are not sure which type to grow, buy seed packets containing mixed lettuce leaves, where you pick the leaves and not the whole plant – these are known as 'cut and come again' salads.

The basics

WHEN TO GROW

Summer through to autumn is the best time to grow lettuce seeds. Sow a few seeds every 5–6 weeks and you will have a healthy supply of lettuce all summer long. This is called successional sowing. If you like, you can move bigger lettuces to a new container to give the others more space.

YOU WILL NEED

- Old colander (metal or plastic) or seed tray, piece of guttering or fruit punnet
- Packet of lettuce seeds
- Multi-purpose or potting compost
- Horticultural grit (small stones) or small handful of gravel
- Water sprayer (use an old cleaning spray bottle, once washed out)

Preparation

BE SOIL READY

Fill the colander or container with the compost. Crumble the soil through your fingers to remove any lumps which may stop the little seedlings from pushing up through the compost. A washed-out old spray cleaning bottle is ideal for keeping the compost damp at all times.

How to grow

SOWING & GROWING

There are lots of tiny lettuce seeds in one packet. Shake a few into the palm of your hand. Scatter the seeds onto the surface of the compost and then sprinkle a dusting of compost to cover lightly. Don't worry about the seeds being close together, you can sort out any overcrowding later.

Water gently using the spray bottle. Within a week, tiny seedlings will appear. Keep moist but don't over water. The best place for the colander is on a bright sunny window sill, in a greenhouse or shed with natural light or in a sheltered sunny spot outside.

Wait for the seedlings to grow a bit more to see if you have sown any too close together. Using a lolly stick as a lever you can lift some carefully out of the compost without damaging the others. These can be replanted in another container. You will want to end up with about five lettuce plants growing in an average sized colander.

HARVESTING

You can pick the salad leaves at any stage. Using your hands, pick off leaves from different plants to ensure that the lettuces grow healthily. You can keep picking leaves for about 6 weeks.

Let's get cooking with lettuce!

Rainbow rolls – page 124
Easy-peasy garden salad – page 119
Squeaky salad – page 120

Little Grower's Tip

Wait until the seedlings have big enough leaves before you remove the overcrowded ones. Always hold seedlings by their leaves not their stems. Stems are too weak and could break easily.

Growing Winter Lettuce

Sow winter varieties in the same way as
summer lettuce and keep on an indoor
window sill or in a sheltered spot outside.
Winter lettuce has a spicy strong taste,
so pick the leaves when they are small
and tender. They will take a little longer
to grow and are smaller than summer
lettuces but they don't need to be watered
much in the winter.

SQUASH IN A TUB

Courgettes and pumpkins are members of the squash family just like butternut squash. They are great eaten raw or can be cooked in lots of different ways – grilled, roasted, fried, barbecued or even baked in a cake. Even the flowers are edible, they are usually fried but you can eat them raw as well, they taste just the same as a courgette. Pick them smaller as they are more tasty, larger ones have a higher water content and less flavour.

Courgettes are some of the easiest vegetables to grow in summer. One plant goes a long way and will produce lots of tender, tasty fruits from midsummer through to autumn. Courgettes don't need as much space as pumpkin and butternut squash, so they are perfect for growing in containers in small spaces. They are fast growing, hungry crops that need warmth and lots of water, so it's best to sow them inside in early summer and plant them outside in midsummer when the weather is warmer.

The basics

WHEN TO GROW

Sow seeds inside in early summer, then repot outside in midsummer.

YOU WILL NEED

- 5–7cm width small yogurt pots or biodegradable pots
- Tray
- Recycled plastic trug/DIY tub with handles or very large pot for final growing
- Courgette, butternut squash or pumpkin seeds or small plants called 'plugs'
- Multi-purpose or potting compost
- A screwdriver or metal skewer
- Plant label (wooden lolly stick), pen or pencil
- Watering can
- Horticultural grit (small stones)
- Liquid seaweed feed (or homemade nettle feed, see page 64)

Preparation

BE SOIL READY

If you are using small plant plugs, you can skip this section and move straight to transplanting.

Once an adult has helped you make holes in the bottom of your yogurt or eco-friendly pots, put your pots on a tray to catch water spills. Fill nearly to the top with compost. Gently tap the pots to remove any air pockets in the soil and add some water to dampen the compost.

How to grow

SOWING & GROWING

Both courgette and pumpkin seeds are large so only place one seed per pot and plant them vertically. Hold the seed up between your thumb and index finger with the pointy end up. Gently push it into the compost, still keeping it upright until it is below the surface of the soil. About ½ inch down is perfect. Sprinkle a little more compost on top to cover it completely. Add a little more water, being careful not to drown the seed. Place your seedlings in a warm and sunny place indoors.

The seeds will start to germinate (begin to grow) within 10 days. You will see two quite large leaves when the seedlings push up through the compost. Try not to let the seedlings dry out. They grow very fast and will use up the water and nutrients in the pots quite quickly. You will eventually need one large container per plant so if you have leftover seedlings, you can give them away to a friend.

TRANSPLANTING

If you are using bought plants, or when your seedlings look as if they are getting too big for the pots, it is time to move them to your bigger container.

If the weather is warming up it is a good idea to place them outside in the sun for a week or two, but remember to bring them in at night. This is called hardening off, and helps your plant to adjust to being outside permanently. In midsummer, or when all risk of cold nights have passed, it should be safe to plant them outside. Choose a sunny spot and prepare your plastic tub. With an adult, make some holes in the bottom using a metal skewer or screwdriver, 7 or 8 should be enough. Fill the tub with compost, adding a handful of grit to help drainage. Make a hole in the compost of each container with a trowel, deep enough for the roots of the plant. Carefully remove your plants from their pots and transplant them straight into the holes. They will look small but they will fill the space very quickly. Courgettes and squashes are hungry plants as they are fast growing, so add a liquid seaweed feed once a week or make your own using nettles, see page 64. Pumpkins need watering daily as they grow much bigger.

HARVESTING

If you have planted courgettes, they will begin fruiting by the middle of summer. It is always best to pick them when they are small as they take less time to cook and are tastier – they can even be eaten raw.

Using a knife or gardening scissors (called secateurs), slice or cut the end of the courgette to release it. Pulling the veggies could cause damage to the main plant. One courgette plant will produce lots of veggies every week. It is important to keep picking the courgettes to encourage more to grow. To harvest pumpkins or butternut squash you will have to wait longer, they need lots of sunshine to ripen and for their skins to harden. The fruits will start to appear by the middle of summer but they won't be ready until the autumn. Perfect timing for Halloween!

Let's get cooking with squashes!

Pumpkin, feta and courgette fritters – page 145
Magical chocolate fudge cake – page 153
Sausage and veggie sleepover – page 108
Ten veg soup – page 140

MAKE A TEE 'PEA'

Homegrown peas and mangetout are the best! Mangetout are just underripe pea pods which you can pick and eat whole. Peas can be eaten raw, straight from their pods or you can cook them. Either way they are sweet, crunchy and taste much better than shop-bought frozen peas. Julia's daughters used to love coming home from school to pick and eat peas straight from their pods in the veg patch. Peas like to climb up a framework, trellis or bamboo canes, so this tee 'pea' will make your peas happy! Peas are easy to grow but you will need to keep the birds off them. Try doing this naturally by using twiggy hazel branches for the structure. The twigs give protection and stop the birds from pecking the peas.

The basics

WHEN TO GROW

Early summer is the best time to start sowing pea seeds, when the soil is beginning to warm up. You don't need lots of space as peas will happily grow in a large pot or tub. One packet of pea seeds contains lots of seeds, so you can sow a few now and some more through the summer months for a later crop. If you don't fancy waiting a few weeks for the pea seeds to germinate, you can buy little pea plug plants from local markets or farm shops.

YOU WILL NEED

- Big, deep tub or large container about 30cm in diameter (a trug/DIY tub is ideal. You will need to make some drainage holes.)
- 5–7 hazel or birch sticks collected from hedgerows or similar long sturdy sticks or canes
- Pea/mangetout seeds or pea plug plants
- Multi-purpose or potting compost
- Horticultural grit (small stones) or gravel
- Garden twine or string
- Screwdriver or skewer to make drainage holes
- Pencil or stick
- Plant label (wooden lolly stick), pencil or pen
- Watering can

Little Grower's Tip

Don't be tempted to pick the pretty pea flowers, you won't get any pea pods if you do this.

Preparation

BE SOIL READY

Ask an adult to help you make 4–5 drainage holes in the bottom of your tub, using a screwdriver or skewer. Choose a sheltered sunny spot for your tub before adding the compost, it will be too heavy to move later. Fill your tub to just below the top with multi-purpose compost mixed with some horticultural grit, if you have any, or gravel for extra drainage. Bury your chosen sticks as deeply and firmly as you can, spaced evenly in a circle around the edge of the tub. The sticks should be as tall as you! The twiggier the stick the better, for the peas to climb up. With one hand, clench the tops of the sticks together and tie garden twine or string around them a few times so that they are securely fastened together. Ask an adult to help you do this.

How to grow

SOWING

Peas can be sown directly into the compost, you will see they are just like dried peas. Place a pea seed next to the base of each stick and push it down into the compost about 5 or 6 cm. If you prefer you can use a pencil or stick to make the holes in the compost. Push back the compost to cover the seeds then give a good watering in. Use the same method for beans. Don't forget to pop a labelled lolly stick by each seed.

GROWING

Peas and beans like lots of water, they are fast-growing, hungry plants. In under two weeks you will see lots of green shoots appearing, just make sure you keep watering and watch them climb to the top of the hazel sticks. To help them start climbing you can tie them to the lower branches with twine. Pinch out the top of the pea plants (these are called tips) when they get to the top of the sticks, this stops them growing any taller and helps put energy back down the stems to produce lots of tasty pea pods. Pea tips are called pea shoots and you can eat them – they taste just like a peas. Runner bean tips are not edible so add them to the compost or discard.

Little Grower's Tip

Add a layer of mulch to the base of the plants, this helps lock in moisture and stops the compost from drying out. Mulch is organic leaf matter. Find out how to make it on page 13.

Little Grower's Tip

Runner beans can also be grown in large deep containers. Why not fill another tub with runner beans seeds or plant peas and beans and see which one scrambles to the top of the hazel sticks first.

Little Grower's Tip

At the end of the season leave a few pea pods on the plants until they are brown and completely crisp and dry. Store them in an airtight container; these will be new seeds for next year. Throw any that look damaged onto the compost heap, as they will not grow properly.

HARVESTING

Once you see the pea flowers, pea pods will soon appear. Pick them small and eat as mangetout or wait until they are full of good size peas and then start picking. Remember the more you pick the more they will grow. Carefully remove the pods first in order to collect the peas. Break the pod open and remove the peas from inside (this is called shelling). If you want to grow more peas in the middle of summer then you must replace the compost and start sowing again, using the same tub. Peas are very hungry plants and will have used up all the nutrients with the first sowing. Runner beans will start to grow a week after you see the flowers.

Let's get cooking with peas!

Easy-peasy summer salad – page 119
Green dip – page 101

Little Grower's Tip

Water your tub every day when it is warm and sunny. Even when it rains, there will not be enough rainwater to reach the roots of your plants.

STRAWBERRY CLOUDS

Instead of flowers in a hanging basket, why not try growing beautiful strawberry plants instead? They look like fantastical fruity clouds and you can pick a cheeky strawberry from the air whenever you like. Freshly picked home-grown strawberries are sweeter and juicier than any fruit you may have tried before. What's more, they are easy to grow and will come back to fruit every summer for about 5–6 years. Strawberries can be grown in pots, the ground or hanging baskets – or all three!

The basics

WHEN TO GROW

Early summer is the best time to start planting strawberries. It is much easier to buy small plants (plugs) than to grow strawberries from seed. Most farm shops, garden centres and markets sell a few varieties of strawberry plants.

YOU WILL NEED

- 3 young strawberry plants
- Multi-purpose or potting compost
- Hessian (fabric)
- Hanging basket frame
- Hooks, brackets and fastenings to attach to a wall or find a strong tree branch to hang the basket from
- Scissors
- Liquid tomato feed
- Watering can

Preparation

MAKE YOUR HANGING BASKET

You can buy hanging baskets all ready to plant but they are easy and fun to put together yourself, here's how:

1. Turn the hanging basket frame upside down on top of your hessian cloth
2. Using scissors, cut a circle round it larger than the hanging basket, leaving enough cloth to hang over the sides.
3. Line the hanging basket with the cloth and tuck any excess fabric inside the framework of the basket. There is no need to make drainage holes as hessian is porous (water can escape).
4. Once made, you can reuse every year!

BE SOIL READY

Put the basket on a flat surface and fill it with multi-purpose compost to the top of the hessian. Keep some liquid feed near the basket as you will need to feed the soil regularly during the fruiting season.

CHOOSE YOUR PLANTS

When choosing your strawberry plants always check they are not too big for their pots with their roots tightly jammed in (this is called pot bound). Healthy plants will have lots of new shoots and green leaves. Avoid plants with yellow, faded or dying leaves and dry soil. Three plants is a good number for one basket.

How to grow

PLANTING & GROWING

Soak the strawberry plants in water before removing them from their small pots. Bury them evenly in the compost to about the same height as they were in their original pots. Make sure this is about 3.5 cm below the top of the hanging basket to allow plenty of room for watering. Thoroughly water them in and allow the water to soak down through the compost before hanging the baskets up. Ask someone to help you hang them as the basket will now be heavy.

Hanging baskets need daily watering and strawberries need a feed once every two weeks. A tomato feed is perfect. You can buy this liquid from any good garden centre. Just follow the instructions on the back of the bottle.

Little Grower's Tip

Hanging baskets can be planted up with other decorative plants once the strawberry season is over, or you could fill them with lettuces that grow through the winter, see page 47.

Little Grower's Tip

When you remove the strawberry plants from their pots, gently tease the roots free, trying not to break any. This gives them a good start in their new home.

HARVESTING

First, the plants will flower. Don't be tempted to pick them as not only will they look pretty in your hanging basket but it's these flowers that turn into strawberries! Pick the strawberries as soon as they turn red. Don't leave them too long or the birds will have a feast!

Let's get cooking with strawberries!

Campfire skewers – page 161
Eton mess ice cream cake – page 173
Strawberry butterfly cakes – page 169
Messy tart – page 174

Little Grower's Tip

Strawberries will produce fruit for up to 5-6 years. Keep plants somewhere sheltered through the winter and don't let them dry out. They will be ready to use next spring.

ANTING!
Autumn

BEETS THE WASHING UP!

You can't beat beetroot and radishes for easy planting. They need little space and will happily grow in a variety of containers, including an old washing up bowl. Just add sunshine and water. You can eat them raw or cooked and in sweet or savoury recipes. Beetroot is especially delicious when combined with chocolate – honestly!

Did you know that beetroot can be red, pink or yellow and that some even have candy stripes? They are best picked when small – the size of a golf ball – when they are more tender and take less time to cook. Radishes are pink, red and white. They add spice and colour to salads and are delicious in stir fries or eaten whole dipped in hummus.

Little Grower's Tip

Beetroot leaves are edible, so pick a few while they are growing to add colour and a tasty beetroot flavour to salads.

The basics

WHEN TO GROW

Although they are usually sown in the spring and summer months, beetroot and radish seeds can also be sown in early autumn. The weather is mild and the soil is still warm from the summer sun, and you will be able to enjoy your harvests through the winter and into next spring. The seeds can be sown directly into their final growing position in the washing up bowl.

YOU WILL NEED

- Multi-purpose or potting compost
- Old washing up bowl, basket or recycled plastic container
- Screwdriver or metal skewer to make drainage holes
- Plant label (wooden lolly stick), pen or pencil
- 1 packet of beetroot seeds
- 1 packet of radish seeds
- Watering can

Preparation

BE SOIL READY

Ask an adult to help you make 4–5 drainage holes in the bottom of the bowl or container using a metal skewer or screwdriver. Fill the washing up bowl to just below the top with multi-purpose or potting compost. Radishes and beetroot are fast, hungry crops so give them an extra boost by adding some homemade compost, if you have some, or locally-sourced farm manure. If you don't have either, you can use a nitrogen plant feed or make your own nitrogen feed using well-soaked nettle leaves. See left.

How to grow

SOWING

Pour a few seeds into your hand. Sow the seeds individually by gently pressing them down with your finger 3cm deep and 6–7cm apart in the compost.

Try sowing radish and beetroot alternately in the same pot. Don't worry if some stick together, you can easily pull one out later. If they come out roots intact you can replant these ones somewhere else.

Scatter a little more compost over the seeds. Keep the compost moist at all times, a little water often is best. Pop labelled lolly sticks into the soil next to the seeds.

GROWING

Within a few days your seeds will start to germinate. You will quickly see if you have sown them too close together but they are easy to pull out. Move your washing up bowl to a sunny spot. Ask an adult or friend to help you as it will be heavy.

HARVESTING

It will take 6 weeks for your radishes to grow to harvesting size and 12 weeks for the first beetroots to appear. You will see the beetroots swell up out of the soil; pull them up by their leaves when they are the size of golf balls. They won't get much bigger but you don't have to harvest them all in one go if you don't want to. You can easily leave some to grow to next spring, just place the bowl in a sheltered spot during colder months. Don't leave radishes too long, though, as they will become too big and tough.

Save The Planet Tip

To make your own plant feed, fill half a bucket with nettle leaves then fill with water. Strain after 1-2 weeks into a bottle. Use one part liquid feed to ten parts water.

Let's get cooking with beetroot and radishes!

Magical chocolate fudge cake – page 153
Rainbow rolls – page 124
Pink dip – page 98

Little Grower's Tip

Allow one or two of your radish plants to flower and produce seeds at the end of the growing season next spring. This is called 'going to seed'. You can dry some of these seeds and save them for next season. Radish flowers are edible too!

SWEETIE PEAS

Pea shoots are easy-peasy to grow! Packed full of vitamins and nutrients they are super healthy, with the taste of the freshest, sweetest pea. They are super-fast growers and as summer harvests fade you can grow your very own supply inside all through the winter. Pea shoots are a healthy fast food. Did you know that pea shoots will grow in compost or just on damp kitchen paper? How clever is that?

The basics

WHEN TO GROW

Sow and grow indoors from autumn through to early spring for a green and plentiful supply of tender, tasty pea shoots.

YOU WILL NEED

* Multi-purpose compost, potting compost or kitchen towel
* Pea seeds, any variety
* Large sweet/biscuit tin or similar (about 15–20cm diameter), 2–3 baked bean tins, a cake tin or a recycled plastic food tray
* Water sprayer (use an old cleaning spray bottle, once washed out)
* Plant label (wooden lolly stick), pen or pencil
* Old plastic food tray (e.g. from fruit)
* Scissors

Save The Planet Tip

If you have some seeds left over, keep them to use next autumn. You can keep seeds and use them for up to 3-4 years, after that they will have a poor germination rate and you will need to buy fresh ones.

Preparation

BE SOIL READY

If your tin is quite deep there is no need to make drainage holes in the bottom. Peas are fast growing seeds but they won't be in the tin for very long, so just be sure not to over water them. Fill the tin with compost. You could add grit or gravel for extra drainage but it's not essential. Pick up and tap the tin a few times on a hard surface to knock out any air pockets. Top up the compost again then lightly water it. If you are growing without soil, use a plastic food tray or lid, line it with 2 sheets of kitchen towel, spray some water to make it damp, ready for the seeds to grow on top.

How to grow

SOWING & GROWING

Carefully cut open the packet and scatter the large, round seeds all over the top of the compost. If you are growing without soil, scatter the pea seeds in exactly the same way onto the damp kitchen towel in the plastic food tray. There will be more seeds than you need in one sowing so fold the packet over and save for another sowing, every 6 weeks. This is called successional sowing, see page 44.

Spray with some more water but do not drown the seeds. Too much water will cause them to rot and die. Lightly dust some more compost over the pea seeds in the tin (this is not essential, it just protects them a little bit) then put the tin or plastic food tray in a sunny, warm place like a windowsill in the kitchen. Pop a plant label (e.g. a lolly stick) into the soil or label the plastic tray.

Within a few days you will see green shoots appearing. In about a week the first shoots will be ready for picking.

HARVESTING

Carefully snip the pea shoots when they are about 7–12cm. Always make sure you leave some leaves on each stem to help them grow again. You will have about three pickings from each sowing. After that the seeds will have run out of energy and will stop producing new tender leaves. You can then throw away or compost the contents of the tin and start again.

Let's get cooking with pea shoots!

Easy-peasy garden salad – page 119

Little Grower's Tip

You can sow the remaining seeds in a large deep tub filled with compost and let them grow into pea plants, see Make a Tee 'Pea' on page 53.

Other seeds to sprout

As well as peas, there are other seeds you can sprout. Have you ever tried sunflower shoots? Sunflower seeds can also be grown for their delicious shoots in exactly the same way as peas. Any variety will do, but it's much better value to buy 'bird feed' sunflower seeds as you get more in a bag than in a seed packet. Once the seedlings have grown to about 6cm and one pair of leaves are open, they are ready for harvesting. Snip off the stems and scatter on salads or add into a juice. They are super healthy, with lots of vitamins packed into two leaves!

Unlike pea shoots, the sunflower shoots can only be harvested once. You must then discard or compost the contents of the container and start sowing again for more tasty leaves, using fresh compost and seeds. Sow some every 3–4 weeks for a continuous supply or try our fun planting idea for sunflowers on page 181.

KNOW YOUR ONIONS

Did you know there are lots of different types of onions that you can grow? Whether big, small, mild or strong flavoured, white or red they are packed full of flavour, and an important ingredient in so many recipes. Onions are super-quick and easy to plant and are happy in pots and containers. Don't worry about them being outside all winter either.

It's much easier to plant onion 'sets'rather than sowing onion seeds. Sets are just baby onions, which are disease resistant. You can buy them from garden centres, farmers' markets or online. They are sold in bags of about 50 sets which should leave you with 50 onions. If you don't want to plant them all, why not share with a friend?

The basics

WHEN TO GROW

Autumn is the best time to plant them. Although you can also plant them in spring too.

YOU WILL NEED

- 1 bag of onion sets, red or white
- Clean window box or planter to fit onto window ledges
- A few large stones
- Multi-purpose or potting compost
- Nitrogen or homemade nettle liquid feed (see page 64)
- Label (wooden lolly stick), pen or pencil
- Stick or pencil
- Watering can

Little Grower's Tip

Birds love to pull out newly planted onion sets so lay a few sticks and twigs on top of your window box or pot to stop the birds from taking them.

Little Grower's Tip

It doesn't matter what your window box is made from - plastic, metal, wood or terracotta - your onions won't mind, just make sure it is deep enough, about 25-30cm is perfect. The onions need room to grow strong roots that hold them steady during the winter.

Preparation

BE SOIL READY

Before you fill your window box with compost, place a few large stones inside the base of the container to help with drainage. Add the compost to just below the top of the container. Gently pat the soil to remove any air pockets and top up the compost if necessary. Now move the window box to a sunny windowsill or table outside, preferably nearby so you remember to water them.

How to grow

SOWING & PLANTING

Once you have chosen your onion sets, tip a few into your hand and make holes 7–12cm apart in the compost using a stick or pencil. The onions need enough room to swell without touching each other, which could cause onion rot.

Hold each onion set upright with the pointy bit at the top and carefully nudge one into each hole, making sure you leave the top of the onion out of the soil. Always keep the pointy bits above soil level. Water little and often; once a week should be fine to stop them drying out.

GROWING

In a few weeks you will see green tips appear; this is a sign that the roots are forming. As soon as it turns really cold the onions will stop growing above ground. As daylight hours increase in late winter the onions will start to get bigger and by spring time they will begin to look like proper onions. Their small green shoots will have grown into tall leaves that look similar to leeks. Step up the watering in springtime, especially if it is hot. Add a nitrogen or homemade nettle liquid feed to your watering can once a week to make them big and strong. By early summer they should look really good and be ready for eating.

HARVESTING

You will know when to harvest your onions as the tall green leaves will start to turn yellow in the summer and flop over. This is nature's way of telling you the onions are ready.

Choose a nice sunny day to dig them up. Using a small garden fork or spade, carefully lift under the soil at the base of the onions and remove them. You can eat them straight away or store them for later use (see right).

Little Grower's Tip

You can plant any leftover onion sets in a spare patch of soil in the garden. Make sure you label them so you don't forget what they are. If you leave some in the ground rather than harvesting them all, they will grow tall and produce pale pink flower heads which the bees love in midsummer.

Little Grower's Tip

If you want to store your onions for later then you will need to dry them. Hang them upside down for 2 weeks or lay them flat on a table somewhere sheltered and dry, like a kitchen windowsill, shed or airing cupboard. They can then be stored in a cool dry place without much light, such as a cupboard or shed, to be used later in the year.

A bright idea

Once you have planted your onion sets you could fill the gaps in between with some edible flower plants, which will look lovely and colourful. Next spring, when they have finished flowering, they can be removed to allow the onions space to get bigger.

Let's get cooking with onions!

Sausage and veggie sleepover – page 108
Cheesy root veg bake – page 111
Pork and apple burgers – page 158

EAT YOUR GREENS!

Save the Planet Tip

Caterpillars and birds do like to nibble on broccoli and kale. Instead of using chemical sprays to keep them away, you can cover the plants with an insect mesh. Most good garden centres sell it. The mesh lets in light and you can water your plants through it.

Green leaves are not just lettuce – kale, broccoli, spinach, pak choi and chard are lovely autumn greens that are also easy to grow. The smaller leaves can be eaten raw, like lettuce, or turned into tasty dishes. Experiment and see which ones you like best. You don't need lots of space, they will grow happily in any large deep container or crate. If you water the container regularly you will have a healthy green feast on your doorstep all winter long.

The basics

WHEN TO GROW

Greens are not just for spring sowing, they can be sown in late summer or early autumn. Farm shops, garden centres and markets all have a choice of autumn greens already grown from seed ('plug' plants), which you can just buy and plant at home. Alternatively, grow your greens from seed. Sow them in late summer while the weather is still warm, directly into your chosen container.

YOU WILL NEED

- Multi-purpose or potting compost
- Winter greens seed packets: chard, pak choi, kale, spinach and broccoli or bought 'plug' plants
- An old wooden apple crate, wine box or similar
- A piece of hessian cloth or horticultural liner (or a black bin bag with holes for drainage)
- Scissors
- Trowel
- Plant labels (wooden lolly sticks), pen or pencil
- Watering can

Preparation

LINE YOUR CONTAINER

Measure the hessian or your chosen liner so it fits snugly in the crate or container. Cut the liner with the help of an adult as you will need to use some sharp scissors. Don't worry if you have spare fabric hanging down, you can fold this inside later. Move the container to its final growing position before filling it with compost – it could be too heavy to move once filled with compost. Make sure you choose a sheltered spot.

BE SOIL READY

Fill the container with compost to just below the top. Rub it between your hands to remove any large lumps then sprinkle with water to make it damp.

How to grow

SOWING

It is a good idea to choose 3 or 4 different types of greens to sow. If you have bought plugs (small plants) then you can skip to the transplanting section. Inside a winter greens seed packet there will be smaller packets containing different seeds. Choose 3–4 varieties, and sprinkle a few seeds from each on top of the damp compost. If you like, you can sprinkle each type in a different area of the crate. Now sprinkle a little more compost on top of the seeds and water them lightly.

GROWING AND WATERING

In about one week your seedlings will start to appear. Pull out any overcrowded ones and either throw them away or plant them in another container or elsewhere in the garden. This is known as thinning out. You don't want any more than 6 plants in a large crate. Plants grown too close together will not grow very big as their roots cannot develop properly. Make sure to water your box when the compost feels dry.

TRANSPLANTING

If you have bought plug plants, carefully remove them from their pots. Make a hole in the compost with a trowel, as deep as the pots they were grown in, and place the plants in each hole. Space them about 15cm apart. Add more compost around the base and water them in.

HARVESTING

Keep watering as the plants grow and once the leaves are big enough (for kale, spinach and chard, this is usually 6 weeks from sowing) you can pick them as and when you need them, always leaving some leaves on each plant. This is known as 'cut and come again'. More leaves will grow in place of the ones you have picked. Pak choi can be picked small or big but it is usually harvested

Little Grower's Tip

Label your seeds with a lolly stick so you don't forget what you are growing and eating!

Little Grower's Tip

If you cut your pak choi plants 1 inch above the base, leaving the root in the ground, they will start to sprout more leaves within a few days.

whole. Broccoli takes longer to grow, depending on the variety. The sprouting types take 15–20 weeks to be ready – from late autumn through to early spring, but they are worth waiting for!

To harvest broccoli, cut the top off the main stem with the central flower head on. Once you have done this lots of florets will start to appear about a week later lower down the stem. Remember the more you pick the more it will grow. As the weather warms up in the spring the florets will start to flower, this means it is the end of the season. Now you can dig up the broccoli plants and compost or discard them.

Let's get cooking with autumn greens!

Kale crisps – page 133
Sticky salmon – page 134
Squiggly noodle soup – page 137
Ten veg soup – page 140

Little Grower's Tip

You can fill a washed out cleaning spray bottle with diluted washing up liquid, and use it to spray the leaves to stop caterpillars eating them.

ANTING!
Winter

EGG FRIENDS

Making these funny little people with their crazy hair is a fun activity for all ages and all times of the year, as they can be grown inside. Garden cress is a herb used in recipes but it is also eaten as a medicine in some countries. The edible shoots have a mild, peppery taste similar to watercress (not surprising considering the two are botanically related and are from the same plant family). Be careful when handling the shells as they are very fragile.

The basics

WHEN TO GROW

Egg friends can be grown all year round, and your egg friend cress 'hair' will appear within 3–4 days. Just keep watering them so they don't dry out.

YOU WILL NEED
- Empty eggshells in halves, preferably large
- Cotton wool to stand eggshells up
- Cardboard egg box
- Multi-purpose or potting compost
- Cress seeds (sometimes called mustard and cress)
- Water sprayer (use an old cleaning spray bottle, once washed out)
- Waterproof felt tip pens or paints
- Kitchen towel

Little Grower's Tip

Cress is a bit of a super-food – it contains lots of vitamins including A and C, plus iron, calcium and potassium, so will help you stay healthy.

Preparation

CHOOSE YOUR CONTAINER

Egg friends are grown in eggshell halves – you should end up with two halves any time you crack an egg. Carefully wash used eggshells in some warm soapy water and let them fully dry out on some kitchen paper. When you have about 6 halves, you will have enough to make an eggshell family.

BE SOIL READY

You need to fill the eggshells with soil before you decorate them, otherwise they will be too fragile.

Stand the halved eggshells in an old egg box, and using a teaspoon, carefully fill each one half way with multi-purpose or potting compost. Pat the soil down lightly and spray with a little water to make them damp, but not soaked. Alternatively, fold up a piece of kitchen paper and tuck that inside the eggshell, then spray with water. The cress will also grow happily on the wet paper.

Wipe the outside of the shells to remove any dirt, then use your felt tips or paints to gently draw some faces on the shells. The cress will be the hair!

Put the eggshells back in the box, making sure you can see their faces (a bit of cotton wool in the bottom will help them stand a bit taller if you need it).

How to grow

SOWING

For each egg friend (half eggshell) carefully tip about ¼ teaspoon of cress seeds into your hand. Sprinkle onto the damp soil or wet paper, and repeat for the rest of your egg friends.

WATERING AND GROWING

Don't let the soil or paper in your eggshells dry out. Spray it lightly every time it feels dry. It's useful to set a time of day to check the soil (after breakfast for example) so you don't forget.

Place your egg box in a light place such as a windowsill or kitchen table. In 3–4 days you will see tiny green leaves appear and these will continue to grow until they are about 4cm long and ready to cut.

HARVESTING

Carefully use a pair of scissors to snip the cress leaves and their stems – make sure you ask for some adult help if you need it.

Make your own lunch!

Why not try an egg and cress sandwich? Mash a chopped up peeled hardboiled egg with 1 heaped teaspoon of mayonnaise and a pinch of salt. Thickly spread onto sliced buttered bread and top with some snipped cress 'hair'. Top with another slice of buttered bread and cut into quarters. Delicious!

Save the Planet Tip

Because garlic has such a strong scent it acts as an organic pest control and helps keep the bugs away. Carrots suffer from pests, so if you are growing carrots as well, make sure you move the boots nearby.

SMELLY FEET

Wellington boots make perfect containers for all sorts of veggies, herbs and flowers, but we think some stinky garlic is the best choice! Garlic comes in many forms and can actually taste quite mild as well as seriously strong, depending on the variety you choose. You can eat garlic raw or cooked and it will ward off not only vampires but colds too!

The basics

WHEN TO GROW

Winter is the perfect time to plant garlic, so you can harvest fat, flavoursome 'heads' (the name for garlic) the following summer. It is said that if you plant garlic on the shortest day it is ready for harvesting on the longest day!

There are lots of varieties to choose from and two different types of garlic, soft neck and hardneck. Hardneck garlic is smaller than softneck but the stems are edible. Softneck does not have edible stems but the cloves are much bigger and they are excellent for storing to use later. Try to choose some grown and produced locally, as you will have the same soil and climate. Otherwise, garden centres and online suppliers are reliable sources.

YOU WILL NEED

- One head of garlic
- Old wellington boots or containers about 25cm deep
- Screwdriver or metal skewer to make holes in the bottom
- Plant label (wooden lolly stick), pen or pencil
- Wooden spoon or stick
- Multi-purpose or potting compost
- Horticultural grit (small stones) or a handful of gravel
- Watering can

Preparation

CHOOSE YOUR CONTAINER

You don't need lots of space to grow garlic. An old wellington boot makes an excellent garlic planter as you can bury your garlic nice and deep. Alternatively, you can use a cut-off milk carton or recycled pot. Ask an adult to help you make some drainage holes in the sole of the boot, not the heel as it is too thick. Garlic will happily grow in any container outside as long as the soil or compost is well drained.

BE SOIL READY

Choose a sunny location and fill your boot or boots with compost. Add a handful of gravel or horticultural grit to help water drain away. Fill the boots to the top and stamp them on the ground to knock out any air pockets.

How to grow

PLANTING

Break up the garlic head into cloves, and try to use the larger cloves for planting. The really small ones won't grow very big, so plant them somewhere else and just use their stalks to add flavour to soups and pasta dishes. The cloves have a top and bottom, the top is usually pointy and the bottom has a hard long edge. Using a wooden spoon handle or stick, make a hole in the soil a little deeper than the clove, but no more than twice its depth. Make holes about 10–15cm apart if you are planting in a larger container. Drop a clove into each hole with the tip pointing upwards. Cover with more compost and water them in. Don't forget to add a label. It is easy to forget what you have planted and where.

WATERING AND GROWING

Place your boots in a sheltered spot, by the back door is ideal so you remember to water them through the winter. Within two weeks you will see bright green tips appear through the soil. Now you can sit back and wait for next summer – garlic is a slow grower but worth it. Water only when the compost looks dry.

HARVESTING

When the leaves start to turn yellow and bend over it's time to lift your garlic. Choose a sunny day, and simply twist the yellowing stems and pull. They should come out of the soil easily. There will be soil on the garlic, don't wash it off. Hang the garlic up somewhere sunny and warm and away from the rain to dry, until the skin is crisp. It can then be stored for use later. Before using, give them a good shake to remove the soil. Freshly harvested garlic is green when peeled but it is still edible.

Let's get cooking with garlic!

Mini but mighty veggie bites – page 104
Cheesy root veg bake – page 111
Sticky salmon – page 134
Squiggly noodle soup – page 137

Save the Planet Tip

Wellington boots are good hand-me-downs but eventually everyone's feet will be too big! They then make excellent planters for small plants such as herbs and edible flowers because they won't rot and can be used time and time again.

Little Grower's Tip

Save a few cloves from one of your garlic heads and leave them to dry on a sunny windowsill in the kitchen. Once dry, store them in an airtight container. They will be your new seed ready for planting next winter.

HERE WE GO ROUND THE BLUEBERRY BUSH

There is nothing better than homegrown blueberries. The good news is their bushes produce heaps of berries, bursting with flavour, every summer without much attention. The berries start growing in the middle of summer and continue through to the autumn, when some leaves turn a gorgeous, rich red colour. You can keep blueberry plants for a number of years and they will carry on producing fruit every summer.

Look out for smaller varieties with more compact bushes as these are perfect for container growing. Blueberries are a superfood, packed full of vitamins and antioxidants and they are delicious and juicy too – especially when picked straight off the bush!

The basics

WHEN TO GROW

Late winter is the best time to plant the blueberry bushes outside as that's when they are dormant (sleeping). Wait for a dry sunny day when it is not too cold.

YOU WILL NEED

- 1 small blueberry plant, either in a pot or bare rooted
- Bag of ericaceous compost (a special compost bought from garden centres)
- Large (30cm+) container, such as a zinc pot, old sink or bath tub. You can also use a large, recycled deep pot or plant straight into the ground
- Garden trowel or fork
- Plant label (wooden lolly stick), pen or pencil
- Horticultural grit (small stones) or gravel
- Watering can
- Netting

Preparation

BE SOIL READY

Choose a sheltered spot with some sun. Blueberries don't need full sun but they will produce bigger berries in a sunny place. Put your container in your chosen spot before filling it with compost or it will be too heavy to move.

Blueberries like acidic soil so you will need a special acidic compost called 'ericaceous'. Fill your chosen container with this compost to just below the top. If your container doesn't have any holes, add a few handfuls of horticultural grit or gravel to help with drainage and make sure not to over water.

How to grow

SOWING

Your blueberry bush will be sold either growing in a pot or as a bare root (not in a pot). You must soak the bare rooted ones overnight in a bucket or watering can before planting. To plant the bush, make a large hole in the middle of the compost. Gently tease the roots apart if they have become tightly knitted together from growing in a pot too long. Carefully place the plant in the hole so as not to damage the roots.

Press down lightly to firm the blueberry plant in place. Add some water but not too much. Try to use rainwater that you have collected instead of tap water, it helps keep the acidity in the compost. Pop in a labelled lolly stick.

WATERING AND GROWING

Blueberries don't need full sun all day and will happily grow in some shade, but do choose a sheltered spot and somewhere not too far away as you must remember to water them often. If the soil looks dry, add water.

HARVESTING

In the late spring you will see tiny blossom flowers appear. This is a sign that small green berries will soon form. They will start to turn blue in midsummer. Once they are dark blue they are ripe and you can pick them. Not all the berries ripen at the same time so keep checking the plants for more berries until the end of the summer.

In the autumn, when you have eaten all the berries and some of the leaves turn a pretty red colour and drop off, it's time to lightly prune (cut back) the bush. Using secateurs with the help of an adult, cut out over-crowded, dead or extra-long branches, as this opens up the middle and will encourage more growth lower down the bush which simply means more berries next year, yum!

Let's get cooking with blueberries!

Blueberry flowerpot muffins – page 170
Messy tart – page 174

Little Grower's Tip

You will need to keep birds away from the ripening berries, so throw some netting (you can buy this from garden centres) over the bush when the berries appear.

GET CO

OKING!

Onions
Root Veggies
Potatoes
Garlic

VEGGIE FRIES

Many of you will have tried making oven baked chips but you may also have discovered how tricky it is to get them really crunchy. This recipe has mastered the art of the crunchy fry! Choose whether you want to make potato, sweet potato, parsnip or carrot fries – or a mix of all!

Serves 4

You will need

600g sweet potatoes, old potatoes (Russet, King Edward and Maris Piper are all good varieties for chips) parsnips or carrots, or a mix
4 tablespoons canola or olive oil

For carrots and sweet potatoes only:
1–2 teaspoons cornflour 600g veggies

Preparation

1. Choose your veggies, peel, core (parsnips) and cut into ½ cm lengths (so they look like thin chips).
2. Old potatoes and parsnips will need soaking in a big bowl of cold water for a minimum of 30 minutes to remove any starch. Then drain and rinse again quickly before draining and drying thoroughly on a tea towel and blotting with kitchen paper. They need to be as dry as possible to make them crunchy.
3. Preheat the oven to 220°C/200°C fan/gas mark 7 (the fan setting is best). Brush 2 tablespoons of oil on a very large flat tray and put into the oven to heat. You can use two trays if you are cooking lots, as they need to have plenty of space.
4. If baking carrots or parsnips, place the dry veggies into a bowl and toss lightly with the cornflour.
5. In a large bowl pour the remaining 2 tablespoons of oil and add 2 teaspoons of sea salt flakes. Add all the veggies and toss together.
6. Spread the veggies over the heated baking tray or trays. They all need to be well spaced apart (or they will steam and not get crunchy!)
7. Bake for 35–45 minutes, turning once or twice during cooking until the fries are crispy. Transfer to a serving bowl.

PINK DIP

The colour of this dip is amazing and it's super easy to make. Serve it with the pitta crisps (see page 101) or vegetable sticks, spoon it next to lamb chops or serve it with the pumpkin fritters on page 145. If you like spice you can add a sprinkling of cayenne pepper or chopped fresh chilli to the mixture. This recipe was inspired by a dish first eaten at Poonie's Kitchen in Sri Lanka.

Serves 4

You will need

5 tablespoons Greek yogurt
½ small raw beetroot (100g), peeled and grated
2 tablespoons pomegranate or pumpkin seeds, plus a few for sprinkling over
1 tablespoon mint leaves, chopped, plus a few leaves to arrange on top
Squeeze of lemon or lime juice
To serve
Raw veggies or pitta crisps

Preparation

1. In a bowl, using a large spoon, mix all the dip ingredients together and season with a pinch of sea salt flakes and some black pepper. Taste, adding more citrus juice if needed.
2. Sprinkle over the remaining mint and pomegranate or pumpkin seeds before serving with raw veggies or the pitta crisps on page 101.

ORANGE DIP

Similar to hummus, this fresh dip is full of vitamins. Adding half a yellow or red pepper is not essential but it adds a lovely flavour. You can also stir in some crumbled feta if you like.

Tahini is a nutty flavoured sesame paste which you can buy from most supermarkets.

Serves 4

You will need

275g mix of carrot, peeled and thickly sliced, and pumpkin or butternut squash, peeled and cut into 3cm cubes
½ red or yellow pepper, deseeded and cut into wedges
2 garlic cloves, kept in their skins
3 tablespoons extra virgin olive oil, plus a little for drizzling
½ tin chickpeas, drained and liquid put aside
¾ teaspoon ground cumin
Juice of ½ lemon
1 heaped tablespoon tahini
50g feta cheese, crumbled, optional

Preparation

1. Preheat the oven to 180°C/160°C fan/gas mark 4.
2. Put the veggies and garlic in a roasting tin and toss with half the oil and some seasoning. Bake for 30–35 minutes, mixing in the drained chickpeas and cumin halfway through cooking. The veggies need to be soft.
3. Put into a food processor or blender (removing the garlic skins first), with the remaining oil, lemon, tahini and 4 tablespoons of chickpea water. Blitz until smooth, then taste for seasoning and blend again. If the mixture seems too thick you can add a little water and blend again. Spoon into a bowl and crumble over the feta if using, then half fold in. Drizzle with a dash more olive oil just before serving.

GREEN DIP

This is a fresh and zesty combination of spring onion, broad beans, avocado and peas.

Serves 4

You will need

2 finely sliced spring onions
1 garlic clove, sliced
1 tablespoon olive oil
125g frozen or podded broad/soya beans
160g frozen or podded fresh peas
2 heaped tablespoons cream cheese
1 avocado, chopped
Juice from 1 lime

Preparation

1. In a pan, soften the spring onion and garlic over a gentle heat with the olive oil. Leave to cool.
2. If using fresh broad beans or peas, cook in salted boiling water for 2–3 minutes. Then drain and rinse in cold water. Frozen veggies just need to be defrosted. Drain thoroughly and deskin the broad beans (soya beans will not need deskinning).
3. Put the veggies and all remaining ingredients, plus the onion and garlic, into a food processor with some ground black pepper and salt. Pulse until just combined but chunky. The dip should not be smooth.

PITTA CRISPS

These are a brilliant store cupboard standby as they keep for ages in a tin and are a great addition to packed lunches or picnics.

Makes 5–6 servings of crisps

You will need

3 pitta breads split widthways to open out
2–3 tablespoons olive oil

Preparation

1. Preheat the oven to 200°C/180°F/gas mark 6. Brush each pitta half on both sides with oil, and sprinkle with salt and pepper. Cut the halved pittas into triangles and arrange on a baking tray.
2. Bake for 7–10 minutes or until golden and crisp
3. Leave to cool then store in an airtight tin.

CRUNCHY, FRUITY, SLAW

We've come up with a fresher, healthier coleslaw which has plenty of crunch. If you'd like a pink version, grate in some raw peeled beetroot. If you hate celery (some do) then just leave it out. This is best mixed just before serving for extra 'crunch'.

Serves 4 adults or 6–8 kids as an accompaniment

You will need

For the dressing
3 tablespoons Greek yogurt
1½ tablespoons olive oil
1 tablespoon cider vinegar (you can add extra for a tangier flavour)
2 teaspoons runny honey or maple syrup

For the coleslaw mix
1 stick celery, thinly sliced
1 large carrot, peeled and coarsely grated
1 apple, peeled, cored and coarsely grated
175g white or Chinese cabbage, finely shredded
Small handful pecan nuts, chopped (optional)
Small handful mixed seeds such as sunflower and pumpkin
Small handful dried cranberries or raisins
1 teaspoon chia seeds (optional)

Preparation

1. In a large bowl mix together the dressing ingredients with a pinch of salt and ground black pepper.
2. Add all the veggies, nuts (if using), fruit and seeds and mix together.
3. Serve straight away to keep everything crunchy.

MINI BUT MIGHTY BAKED VEGGIE BITES

These easy, cheesy vegetarian fingers are a favourite for suppers, picnics and lunchboxes. You can add some cooked chopped bacon to them if you like. When cooking with leeks you must wash them very well once sliced as their layers can contain a lot of soil. Serve them with some ketchup for a picnic or add some baked beans or salad for lunch or dinner.

Makes 8 veggie bites

You will need

120g chopped leek, which is about 2 medium sized leeks, white part only
1 medium sized carrot, peeled and coarsely grated
40g butter
1 large garlic clove, crushed
75g fine brown breadcrumbs (it's best to use an uncut loaf which is a day or two old rather than fresh sliced bread, which won't be dry enough)
100g coarsely grated Cheddar, or another hard cheese
½ heaped teaspoon English mustard
1 large egg, beaten
Light flavoured oil such as rapeseed or vegetable oil for greasing

Preparation

1. Wash the chopped leek and drain well. In a saucepan, melt the butter and add the leeks and the carrot. Fry gently for 8–10 minutes until soft, stirring every so often. Be careful not to turn them brown. Add the garlic for the final minute of cooking. Then cool for 5 minutes.

2. In a big bowl, mix the veggies and all their cooking butter with the breadcrumbs, cheese, mustard, egg, two pinches of sea salt flakes and plenty of black pepper (this is when to add in your cooked chopped bacon if using). Stir together.

3. Preheat the oven to 200°C/180°C fan/gas mark 6. Using clean wet hands, take handfuls of the mixture and form into 8 plump sausage shapes (about 6–8 cm long). Grease a baking tray with a little oil, then place the veggie bites on the tray. Bake for 25 minutes until golden. Cool for 5 minutes before transferring to a plate. Serve with tomato ketchup (see page 150) some baked beans or salad.

HEDGEHOG POTATOES

Some scrumptious potatoes with a spiky personality! Slicing them makes them quicker to cook and also makes the edges wonderfully crispy. Great with a roast chicken or a barbecue. You can also make larger 'daddy' hedgehogs with baking potatoes. Just cut the larger potatoes into hedgehogs then boil in salted water for 5 minutes before drying and brushing with the oil. The addition of cream cheese and Parmesan makes them even more delicious, but you can just serve them undressed if you prefer.

Makes 12

You will need

12 biggish new potatoes
2 tablespoons olive oil
12 teaspoons cream cheese, optional
1 tablespoon grated Parmesan, optional

Preparation

1. Preheat the oven to 200°C/180°C fan/gas mark 6. To slice into each potato without going all the way through, place two chopsticks or spoons vertically on either side, then slice across horizontally. Make small slices about 5mm apart and only ¾ of the way through so that the potatoes remain intact.
2. Put them into a baking dish and pull the slices apart a little bit, so that the oil gets down into them. Mix the oil with ½ teaspoon of sea salt flakes and some pepper then brush the potatoes all over. Sprinkle with a little extra salt (if you like) and bake for 30–40 minutes or until crisp and brown (daddy hedgehogs might take a little longer). Top each with a teaspoonful of cream cheese and a sprinkling of Parmesan.

SAUSAGE & VEGGIE SLEEPOVER

This is what's known as a throw together recipe. It's chock-full of flavour and nutrients. You can halve the amounts for smaller numbers, double them for bigger (cook on two trays) and swap anything you don't like for something that you do: sweet potato in place of pumpkin, broccoli in place of beans – pretty much anything goes!

Serves 4

You will need

8 sausages
½ large or 1 small onion, peeled and cut into wedges
600g new potatoes, halved if larger
Sprig or two of rosemary, bashed, or ½ teaspoon oregano
8 garlic cloves, unpeeled
2½ tablespoons mild oil such as rapeseed or light olive oil
300g pumpkin or butternut squash, peeled and cut into 2cm thick slices
1 red pepper, cored, deseeded and cut into wedges
16 cherry tomatoes
350ml vegetable or chicken stock, made with just-boiled water so it is hot when added
1 heaped teaspoon grainy mustard
150g green beans, trimmed and halved
2 tablespoons parsley (optional)

Preparation

1. Preheat the oven to 220°C/200°C fan/gas mark 7. Put the first six ingredients into a very large baking tray and toss together with some salt and pepper. Put it onto a high shelf and bake for 20 minutes.
2. Reduce heat to 200°C/180°C fan/gas mark 6, remove the tray and stir in the pumpkin, peppers and tomatoes. Bake for a further 10 minutes.
3. Mix the hot stock with the mustard, and add to the tray along with the beans, give everything another stir and bake for a further 10–15 minutes or until veggies are cooked. Sprinkle with parsley, if using, and serve.

CHEESY ROOT VEG BAKE

A nice hearty one for a rainy day. As well as the veggies mentioned below, you could also use sliced sweet potato, pumpkin and beetroot. Just cook until tender. You could also mix some fresh spinach or trimmed kale leaves into the creamy veg just before pouring into the dish.

Serves 4–6

You will need

40g butter
½ large onion, peeled and sliced
1 large parsnip or two smaller ones
1 medium carrot
3 medium potatoes
2 garlic cloves, peeled and sliced
200ml double cream
200ml milk
2 tablespoons grated Parmesan
100g grated cheddar

Preparation

1. Preheat the oven to 180°C/160°C fan/gas mark 4. Melt the butter and add the onion. Soften gently for 8–10 minutes, stirring every so often.
2. Meanwhile peel the parsnip, carrot and potatoes and thinly slice to 5mm thick. Add to the softened onion, with the garlic. Fry gently, stirring regularly for 10 minutes before adding the milk and cream, with a good grinding of pepper and 2 good sized pinches of salt.
3. Bring the liquid to a simmer then let the vegetables gently cook in the milk and cream for 10–15 minutes, stirring every so often, until just tender but not soft. Add the Parmesan and half the cheddar and stir together. Pour into a ovenproof dish and top with the remaining cheese. Bake for 30–45 minutes or until the veggie bake is brown and bubbling and the vegetables are cooked through. You can check whether it is done by sticking a knife into the centre. If the veggies don't feel soft, just bake for a few more minutes.

GARDENER'S CAKE

A delicious and beautiful cake for those who've worked hard in their garden and deserve a treat. Don't be put off by the use of parsnip – this honestly tastes like carrot cake! See if anyone can guess the vegetables and fruits you used – bet they can't! It's also refined sugar free, if you use maple syrup and coconut sugar, which is a big thumbs up. Our preference is to use honey in the icing. Fresh blueberries are also a lovely decoration if you don't have flowers to hand.

Makes one 8 inch cake, 10–12 slices

You will need

120g finely grated parsnip (peeled and trimmed weight)
120g finely grated carrot (peeled and trimmed weight)
120g peeled, cored and grated eating apple (about 1 large or 2 small apples)
50g pecans or walnuts, chopped
150ml mild oil such as rapeseed, sunflower or vegetable
100g coconut sugar or soft brown sugar
100ml maple syrup
4 eggs
1 teaspoon good quality vanilla extract
2 tablespoons orange juice
250g wholegrain stoneground spelt flour
4 level teaspoons baking powder

For the icing
175g slightly softened butter
225g full fat cream cheese
3–5 tablespoons mildly flavoured runny honey or maple syrup

To decorate
Edible flowers and herbs such as lavender, roses, borage, nigella, mint, rosemary, nasturtiums, viola, cornflowers or fresh blueberries

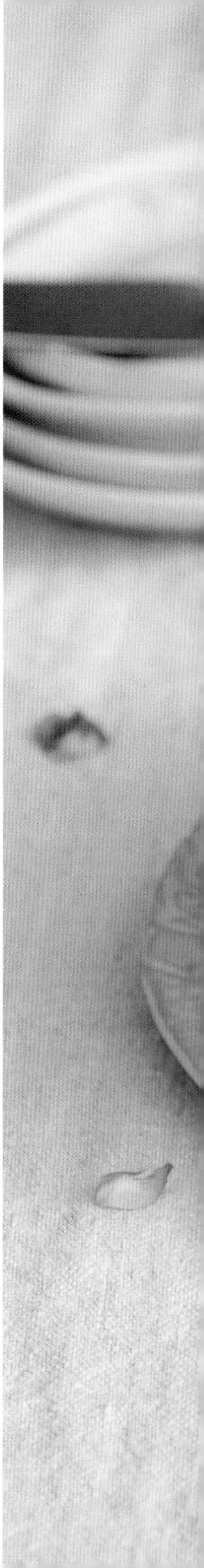

Preparation

1. Preheat the oven to 170°C/150°C fan/gas mark 3.
2. Grate the vegetables and apple and mix together, with the nuts, in a bowl.
3. Put the oil, sugar, maple syrup, eggs, vanilla and orange juice into a mixing bowl and whisk well for a minute or so.
4. Add the grated vegetables, apple and nuts and using a large metal spoon, fold in.
5. Sieve over the flour (you will need to add the grainy bits back into the bowl once sieved), 2 pinches of fine salt and the baking powder. Using the same spoon, gently fold in until just combined.
6. Spoon into a greased and lined deep, loose bottomed 20cm cake tin (or a silicone cake tin).
7. Bake for 55 mins – 1 hour or until cooked through (push a skewer into the centre of the cake – if it's cooked it will come out clean). If it's not quite done, simply return to the oven for an extra 5–10 minutes. Remove from the oven, and after 5 minutes cooling, turn out onto a wire rack to cool.
8. Whisk the butter and cream cheese until smooth then whisk in 3 tablespoons of honey or maple syrup. Add extra if you like it sweeter.
9. Cut the cake in half horizontally (into two layers) then spread over a heaped tablespoon of the cream cheese mixture. Put the cake back together and transfer to a plate.
10. Spoon the remaining icing on top of the cake and carefully smooth over the top and sides. Note: for a more professional look, spread over half of the icing first then chill in the fridge for 10 minutes before spreading over the rest. (The first layer is the crumb coat which covers the cake and any crumbs).
11. Chill in the fridge for 10 minutes, then decorate with herbs and edible flowers and their leaves or blueberries. This cake will keep in the fridge for two days, just bring up to room temperature before serving.

Salad Leaves
Herbs
Edible Flowers

EASY-PEASY GARDEN SALAD

A sweet and lively salad that makes use of the wonderful veggies you can grow in the summer months. It is delicious with griddled or barbecued chicken or salmon (if you leave out the Parmesan).

Serves 4

You will need

2 tablespoons light olive oil or rapeseed oil
2 thick slices sourdough or farmhouse bread, cut into cubes
2 eggs, optional
12 spears asparagus, trimmed
Small handful raw peas
2 tablespoons Parmesan shavings
100g soft lettuce leaves
Handful of pea shoots
2 teaspoons snipped chives, plus flowers

For the dressing
3 tablespoons extra virgin olive oil or rapeseed oil
Good squeeze of lemon juice
¼ teaspoon sugar

Preparation

1. Preheat the oven to 200°C/180°C fan/gas mark 6. Pour the oil into a bowl. Season the oil with sea salt flakes and pepper and toss with the bread cubes. Spoon out onto a baking sheet and bake for 8–12 minutes or until crunchy. Then leave to cool.
2. While the bread cubes are cooking, bring a pan of water to the boil and add the eggs, if using. Boil for 8 minutes, adding the asparagus for the final 1–2 minutes then drain thoroughly. Place the eggs and asparagus in a bowl of very cold water to cool them down quickly. When cool, peel the eggs and cut into wedges.
3. In a large bowl whisk together the dressing ingredients with a sprinkling of sea salt flakes and ground black pepper. Then taste, adding extra lemon juice or sugar as needed. Add the raw peas, most of the Parmesan flakes, lettuce, pea shoots, asparagus, croutons and chives and toss together. Transfer to a plate and top with the eggs, extra Parmesan and chive flowers.

SQUEAKY SALAD

This is a very kid-friendly salad as most children love squeaky halloumi cheese, and the combination with sweet nectarine and salty bacon is a winner.

Serves 4

You will need

1 tablespoon pumpkin seeds
4–6 slices streaky bacon
1 pack halloumi cheese, sliced into 1cm slices
2 ripe nectarines or peaches, de-stoned and cut into wedges
4 little gem lettuces, cut lengthways into wedges

For the dressing
3 tablespoons extra virgin olive or rapeseed oil
2 tablespoons lemon juice
1 teaspoon runny honey

Preparation

1. Preheat a frying pan. Dry fry the pumpkin seeds until toasted then set to one side in a bowl. Put the bacon into the pan and cook on both sides until crispy, and then move it to a plate lined with kitchen paper. When the bacon has cooled slightly, carefully snip into smaller pieces using scissors.
2. Add the halloumi slices to the pan and cook for 2–3 minutes on both sides until golden. Add to the plate with the bacon.
3. In a large bowl, mix the dressing ingredients with a sprinkling of sea salt flakes and ground black pepper. Taste, adding extra lemon juice or honey as needed. Add the nectarine or peach slices and lettuce and toss together. Spoon onto a plate and top with the halloumi, bacon and pumpkin seeds.

MINT & RASPBERRY LEMONADE

Once you have tried homemade lemonade you won't want to buy it ever again. You can flavour it with raspberries or strawberries, depending what you have ready to pick in the garden. You can also use a mix of oranges, lemons and/or limes without the berries for a St Clements. If you prefer sparkling lemonade, just steep the lemons in the 300ml water, then strain into a jug and add 550ml chilled sparkling water when ready to drink.

Makes approximately 1 litre

You will need

5 lemons
3–5 tablespoons caster sugar (or you can sweeten with a natural sweetener such as stevia powder or raw honey, if you prefer)
850ml water
5 raspberries or strawberries, chopped
Handful of mint leaves

Preparation

1. Put the lemons into a pan of boiling water and simmer gently for 8–10 minutes to soften them up, then remove carefully to a plate. When they have cooled down, press and roll them on the work top, then cut in half and juice them into a large bowl or jug. Cut the halved skins in half again to make quarters.
2. To the juice, add 3 tablespoons of sugar, 300ml of boiling water, the quartered lemon skins, raspberries or strawberries and mint.
3. Using the end of the rolling pin, gently squash the fruits down to mix them together. Stir well, then taste for sweetness, adding more sugar if needed (it will taste strong as you haven't added the extra water yet).
4. Pour in 550ml of cold water, stir and chill to steep (if you prefer to use sparkling water then chill the juice first before adding 550ml fizzy water just before serving).
5. Strain through a sieve into a large jug filled with some ice and serve.

RAINBOW ROLLS

Rice paper wrappers start off crisp, but as soon as you dip them in water they soften. You can fill the soaked wrappers with all of your favourite veggies and herbs, and if you like, add some thin cooked rice noodles, chopped chicken, sausage or prawns. Be as adventurous as you dare! They are great for packed lunches. Just place them in a container between lettuce leaves to stop them sticking or drying out. Plastic wrap is not planet friendly and will also stick to the rolls.

Makes 6 long rolls, which you can cut in half

You will need

25g rice vermicelli noodles (optional)
6 spring roll rice wrappers such as Blue Dragon, found in larger supermarkets, oriental shops or online.
A selection of your favourite veggies cut into fine strips or grated, such as cucumber, carrot, red pepper, apple, avocado, sweetcorn, tomato, lettuce or radish, plus, if you like, finely shredded chicken or sliced cooked prawns
1 tablespoon fresh mint and/or coriander, roughly chopped
1 tablespoon chopped roasted peanuts, optional

For the mild chilli dipping sauce
1 lime, juiced
3 teaspoons mild runny honey
1½ tablespoons rice wine vinegar
1 tablespoon fish sauce
1 garlic clove, crushed
½ red chilli, deseeded and finely chopped (optional)

For the peanut dipping sauce
90g crunchy peanut butter
2 tablespoons rice wine vinegar
1½ tablespoons soy sauce
½ garlic clove, crushed
½ teaspoon grated ginger
3 tablespoons coconut milk or water
1 tablespoon runny honey
½ lime, juice only

Preparation

1. Form a line of little bowls containing the filling ingredients you have chosen. If you are using noodles, put them into a bowl and cover with boiling water, leave for 4 minutes, then drain, before cutting with scissors into easy to pick up clumps.

2. Follow the instructions on the packet for soaking the wrappers. Usually this is just dipping the wrapper in a shallow bowl of warm water. Once soft, place the wrapper on a board in front of you. Choose from the ingredients, placing small mounds onto the wrapper in a line. Once you have filled the rolls (enough to make a sausage shape as in the photo on page 125), just pull up each side to cover each end and roll the wrapper and its fillings very tightly. Cut each roll in half and store between lettuce leaves until ready to eat.

3. For the dipping sauces – choose both or just one. Simply stir the ingredients together in a small bowl. For the peanut sauce, add 1–2 tsp water so that the sauce isn't too thick. The sauces will keep in the fridge for up to a week.

4. To serve, place the rolls on a big plate with the sauces on the side for dipping.

THE BEST PESTO FOR KIDS

Nut free, mild in flavour and so delicious that you will want to eat it by the spoonful! Try it in the Pesto pasta salad recipe on page 138 or spoon it over hot new potatoes.

Makes one small jam jar of pesto (like a normal pesto jar size)

You will need

25g basil leaves (this is the weight of leaves only not stem) or ⅔ basil leaves and then the rest baby spinach – this gives a milder flavour
2 tablespoons sunflower seeds
1 small garlic clove, sliced
A good squeeze of lemon juice
125ml extra virgin olive oil or a mix of extra virgin and cold pressed rapeseed for a milder flavour
40g grated Parmesan

Preparation

1. Put the basil, seeds, garlic, lemon, some ground pepper and a pinch of salt into a processor. Whizz, while adding the oil in a slow steady stream. You might need to stop and scrape down the sides.
2. Once all of the oil has been added and the pesto is smooth, add the Parmesan and pulse until combined. Taste, adding a squeeze more lemon or extra seasoning, if needed. Store in a jar in the fridge for 2–3 weeks, covered with a little extra oil, or freeze in ice cube trays and use as required.

FLOWER PETAL SHORTBREADS

You will need

110g plain flour, plus a little for dusting
50g cornflour
50g icing sugar
110g cold butter, cubed
Zest of half a lemon (optional)
Edible flowers, herbs such as mint leaves, or lemon zest for decorating
Caster sugar for dusting

Pretty as a picture, both before and after cooking, these shortbread biscuits are a wonderful way to learn about edible and non edible flowers. Roses, lavender, nasturtiums, violas and herb leaves are all edible and suitable for pressing into sweet or savoury biscuits. Thank you to our favourite flower Amy for sharing her Scottish shortbread recipe.

Makes 16–18 biscuits

Preparation

1. Sieve the plain flour, cornflour and icing sugar into a bowl or food processor. Add the zest, if using, and the butter. Then, either rubbing in using your fingers or pulsing in the food processor, bring the mixture together into a dough. If using your hands, once the butter is completeley rubbed in, squeeze the mixture together to make a dough. Put on a plate, flatten slightly, cover and chill for 15 minutes.
2. Preheat the oven to 180°C /160°C fan/gas mark 4. Place a large piece of baking paper on the work surface and sprinkle with a little plain flour. Place the dough in the middle and top with more paper. Roll out the dough until it is about 1cm thick. Remove the paper (you will need it again), and using circle, star or other shaped cookie cutters, cut out shapes from the dough.
3. Using your fingertips, gently press petals, lemon zest, herb sprigs or whole flower heads into the centre of each shape. Place the piece of baking paper back on top and very gently roll over the flowers with a rolling pin to seal them into the dough. Remove the top sheet, and place on a baking tray. Then carefully, using a blunt knife, transfer the shortbreads to the paper-lined tray, 2cm apart. Chill again for 10 mins.
4. Bake for 10–15 minutes then remove from the oven and sprinkle with caster sugar before cooling on a rack.

For cheese and rosemary or poppyseed shortbreads
Put 150g spelt flour into a bowl or food processor with 100g of Parmesan
cheese, 2 teaspoons finely chopped rosemary needles (or 1 teaspoon
poppy seeds). Add 120g cubed cold butter, and rub together or pulse. Press
together to form a dough and roll out and bake as per the instructions
opposite (don't sprinkle with sugar). Sage leaves, rosemary or dill/parsley
sprigs are great toppings.

Broccoli
Pak Choi
All Things Green

BROCCOLI TREES WITH GARLIC CRUMBS

Broccoli is actually a flower head covered in small, unopened buds. Try using bagels for breadcrumbs instead of bread as they have a slightly sweeter flavour, which is delicious with broccoli. To make breadcrumbs, it's best to use 1–2 day old bread or bagels. Just whizz broken up pieces in a food processor until crumbs form. This recipe is particularly good served with a lemony roast chicken.

Serves 4

You will need

3 tablespoons olive oil
1 large garlic clove, crushed
3 tablespoons coarse bagel or brown breadcrumbs
Large head of broccoli cut into smallish florets
½ red chilli sliced thinly, optional
½ lemon, juice and finely zested

Preparation

1. Preheat the oven to 220°C/200°C fan/gas mark 7.
2. Mix the olive oil with the crushed garlic and some salt and pepper.
3. Add half of the garlic oil to the bagel crumbs. Wash the broccoli and dry completely using kitchen paper before mixing it with the other half of the oil.
4. Spread the broccoli out over a baking paper-lined or non-stick baking tray and bake on a high shelf for 8 minutes.
5. Sprinkle the breadcrumbs and the chilli (if using) over the half-baked broccoli and bake for a further 10–12 minutes or until the breadcrumbs are crisp and brown. Transfer to a serving dish and sprinkle over the lemon juice and zest before serving.

KALE CRISPS

These are really tasty so make plenty. The great thing is that they are healthy too as they contain lots of superfood goodness. A brilliant snack for hungry kids. De-stemming kale is easy. Just run your fingers down the stems and the leaves will break off. Make sure the kale is completely dry before baking.

You will need

200g fresh kale leaves (destemmed weight)
torn into 8cm pieces
1 tablespoon light olive oil or another mild-flavoured oil
½ teaspoon soft brown sugar

Preparation

1. Preheat the oven to 180°C /160°C fan/gas mark 4 (fan setting will give best results).
2. Line two flat baking trays with baking paper.
3. Wash the kale leaves and dry completely using kitchen paper then place into a bowl and toss with the oil and one teaspoon sea salt flakes.
4. Spread the leaves over the two trays, spacing well apart. Bake in the oven for about 10 minutes, keeping a close eye so they don't burn. The leaves should still be green.
5. Remove from the oven and sprinkle with the sugar. Then bake again for a further 2–3 minutes before removing and leaving on the side to crisp up. Toss together and serve immediately.

STICKY SALMON

Everyone loves this, especially if served with a big bowl of noodles.
If you can, use tenderstem broccoli, as it looks prettier and the
salmon sits better on the top. If using a head of broccoli just snuggle
the florets in between the salmon. Trimmed asparagus would also be
a lovely addition.

Serves 4

You will need

1 decent sized bunch (about 250g) tenderstem broccoli, trimmed,
or one head of broccoli, cut into florets
4 x 125–150g skin-on, sustainably sourced salmon fillets
1½ tablespoons soy sauce, preferably reduced salt
2 tablespoons ketchup
4 tablespoons orange juice
3 tablespoons light brown sugar or runny honey
2 tablespoons lemon juice
3–4 cm knob ginger, peeled and cut into strips
2 garlic cloves, thinly sliced

Preparation

1. Preheat the oven to 180°C/160°C fan/gas mark 4.
2. Rinse the broccoli and while still damp put onto a baking tray. Season the
   salmon fillets and sit them on top, skin side up. Put into the oven for about 12
   minutes. (The broccoli will still be quite crunchy after cooking. If you prefer
   it softer you can boil it for a minute before placing it in the base of the tin.)
3. Meanwhile, heat all the remaining ingredients in a pan up to a gentle simmer.
   Let them bubble for a minute or so then set aside until the salmon has finished
   its time in the oven.
4. Pour the sauce over the salmon and broccoli and return to the oven for 5
   minutes or until bubbling. Serve with noodles or rice.

SQUIGGLY NOODLE SOUP

A warming, filling soup full of goodness. Perfect for filling a thermos to guzzle on a picnic, but be sure to snip the noodles with some scissors when cooking, for easier eating on the move.

Serves 4

You will need

1.5 litres well-flavoured chicken stock, preferably homemade
3 spring onions, white part finely sliced, tops reserved and chopped
Small bunch coriander, root and stem roughly chopped, leaves chopped
1 large garlic clove, sliced
5cm piece of ginger, sliced
1 lemongrass stalk (optional), bashed with a rolling pin
1 tablespoon soy sauce
2 teaspoons lemon or lime juice
1 teaspoon coconut or brown sugar
200g thin egg or rice noodles
220g leftover shredded, cooked chicken
3 small pak choi heads, sliced into quarters lengthways
2 teaspoons sesame oil

Preparation

1. Put the stock into a pan with the sliced white spring onion, coriander roots and stem, garlic, ginger and lemongrass, if using. Simmer very gently, with a lid ¾ covering for about 15–20 minutes then strain. Pour the stock back into the pan and throw away the ginger etc.
2. Heat the stock until simmering, then add the soy sauce, lemon or lime juice and sugar. Add the noodles and cook according to the packet instructions. Using tongs, divide the noodles between four bowls.
3. Add the chicken and pak choi to the stock in the pan and cook for 1–2 minutes or until the greens are cooked but crunchy. Using tongs, lift out the chicken and greens and place on top of the noodles. Pour over the stock, then garnish with the spring onion tops and chopped coriander leaves. Drizzle over the sesame oil.

PESTO PASTA SALAD

A fresh pesto based pasta salad is a winner and all the ingredients added to this one are kid-friendly. Obviously if there's something you don't like just add something else instead. Sweetcorn, peas, chopped red pepper, cooked asparagus, chicken, crispy bacon all work! This one lasts a good few days and can cope with being out of the fridge for an hour or three, as long as it's not a scorching day. You can use any green beans for this but just adjust the cooking time if they are thicker. If you want a nut-free version, use the pesto recipe on page 127 and omit the pine nuts.

Serves 6–8

You will need

150g red and yellow cherry tomatoes, halved
300g orzo or risoni pasta
125g fine green beans, trimmed and halved
4 tablespoons pesto sauce, preferably fresh – see recipe on page 127
2 tablespoons lemon juice
2 tablespoons extra virgin olive oil
150g cucumber, cut into chunks
75g pitted green or black kalamata olives, halved
125g mini mozzarella balls (known as bocconcini), halved
5 x 1cm thick slices salami such as milano, cut into chunks, optional
1½ heaped tablespoon toasted pine nuts
2 big handfuls rocket or spinach leaves (optional)
1 tablespoon chopped chives
Torn basil leaves and edible flower petals, if available, to serve

Preparation

1. Preheat the oven to 180°C/160°C fan/gas mark 4.
2. Put the halved cherry tomatoes into a dish and bake for 10 minutes or until softened a little.
3. Meanwhile, cook the pasta in a large pan with plenty of salted boiling water for the cooking time stated on the packet. You will need to give it a good stir every so often as it can stick a bit. Add the green beans for the final 2 minutes so that they are cooked but still have some 'crunch'.
4. Drain the pasta and beans thoroughly (keep a little of the pasta water in a cup) then transfer to a bowl and while still hot stir in the pesto, lemon juice, olive oil and some sea salt flakes and ground black pepper to taste. Leave to cool.
5. If the pasta is a little dry, add a small splash of pasta water to loosen. Stir in the cooled tomatoes, cucumber, olives, mozzarella, salami (if using), pine nuts, chives and rocket or spinach (optional). Sprinkle with torn basil and flower petals, if available.

TEN VEG SOUP

This will give you 'souper powers' as it contains ten veggies, if you count the herbs. It's a great 'keep everyone going' recipe. A good one to pop into a thermos too. Kids love grating over lots of fresh Parmesan and tearing off hunks of bread to dip in, so just put the bread, grater and cheese on the table and let everyone pile in. You can add nj,cannelini, borlotti or butter beans if you fancy and if there's a veggie you don't like just leave it out or swap it for another.

Serves 6–8

You will need

1 stick celery, finely chopped
½ large or 1 small onion, peeled and finely chopped
1 medium carrot, scrubbed and finely chopped
2 garlic cloves, peeled and chopped
2 tablespoons extra virgin olive oil, plus a drizzle more
2 slices smoked bacon, finely chopped (optional)
1 medium courgette, grated
1 medium potato, peeled and chopped
1.5 litres vegetable stock
1 x 400g tin chopped tomatoes or 4 large ripe tomatoes, cored and chopped
½ teaspoon dried oregano or 1 teaspoon fresh oregano leaves
2 tablespoons baby pasta such as risoni or crushed vermicelli
2 handfuls chopped kale, shredded cabbage or baby spinach leaves
2 tablespoons chopped basil leaves
Grated Parmesan and bread to serve

Preparation

1. Chop the first four ingredients. You can save time by using a food processor. Leave the bacon, kale, cabbage or spinach and potatoes to chop by hand.
2. In a large pan heat the oil and gently fry the celery, onion, carrot, garlic and bacon, if using, with ½ teaspoon of sea salt flakes, stirring occasionally.
3. After 10 minutes add the courgettes, tomatoes, potatoes, stock and oregano and a grinding of black pepper. Cover and simmer for about 15 minutes.
4. Add the pasta and cook for a further 6–7 minutes then add the kale, cabbage or spinach and keep cooking until the pasta is just tender. Taste for seasoning (you might need extra salt if you haven't used smoked bacon) and serve sprinkled with basil, Parmesan, a drizzle of oil and some crusty bread.

Pumpkins

Courgettes

Cucumbers

Tomatoes

PUMPKIN, FETA & COURGETTE FRITTERS

You will need

300g peeled pumpkin or
butternut squash, grated
300g courgette, grated
2 garlic cloves, crushed
4 spring onions, finely
chopped
3 eggs
About 75g wholegrain spelt
flour (or plain/wholemeal
flour)
200g feta, crumbled
½ teaspoon garam masala or
fresh dill, chopped
3-4 tablespoons olive oil

To serve
Tzatziki or the pink dip on
page 98

These tasty little fritters make a brilliant packed lunch, with cucumber sticks. They also go well with a tzatziki dip or try the pink dip on page 98. Garam masala is a spice blend which adds delicious flavour but not spicy heat. If you aren't keen on spices, you can add a teaspoon of chopped fresh dill instead. It's best to make the mixture just before cooking, or the veggies will let out some of their natural water and it will become too wet.

Makes 14–16 fritters

Preparation

1. Put the pumpkin and courgette into a bowl and scrunch in about ¾ teaspoon of salt flakes. Stir together then leave for 20 minutes.
2. Transfer the pumpkin/courgette mixture to a sieve and, over a sink, use your hands to squeeze the vegetables so some of the water drains away. This stops the fritters becoming too soft.
3. Return the vegetable mixture to the bowl and add the remaining ingredients as well as some ground black pepper. Stir together. The mixture should be stiff enough that they can hold their shape in the frying pan. Add a little extra flour if needed.
4. Heat 2 tablespoons oil in a frying pan. When hot, add a heaped tablespoon of the mixture to make each fritter, flatten slightly as shown in the picture. Fry for about 3 minutes on each side over a low–medium heat, until the fritters are nice and brown. Serve with a spoonful of tzatziki or the pink dip on page 98.

TERRIFIC TRAY BAKE PIZZA

This recipe proves cooking can be faster than a takeaway; it makes a brilliant five-minute pizza dough. You don't even need to weigh the ingredients out. Go traditional, melting the cheese as you cook the pizza, or 'Summer Style', just tearing cold mozzarella over the hot pizza and scattering over some basil and rocket. Salami, pepperoni or ham, sliced mushrooms, olives and sweetcorn are also delicious additions to decorate the pizza with before cooking. We've included a fun recipe for 'pizza snails' too.

Makes one tray (about 6–8 big pizza slices)

You will need

For the quick pizza dough
375g self-raising flour, and extra for dusting
300g Greek yogurt
2 tablespoons extra virgin olive oil

For the topping
150ml homemade tomato ketchup (page 150), pizza sauce or passata, mixed with ¼ teaspoon dried oregano (or half teaspoon fresh), salt and pepper and 1 tablespoon extra virgin olive oil
350–400g mixed tomatoes (approx. 10 medium tomatoes), sliced thinly (optional)
2 balls mozzarella, drained and torn
8–10 basil leaves, torn and/or a handful rocket leaves

Preparation

1. Put the dough ingredients plus 1 teaspoon of sea salt flakes into a bowl and mix together using a blunt knife until they form a rough dough. Using your hands, bring the dough together. If it seems too dry, keep kneading as it will eventually come together.
2. Transfer to a floured surface and continue to knead for 3–4 minutes until smooth.
3. Preheat the oven to 200°C/180°C fan/gas mark 6.
4. Grease a shallow-lipped, large baking tray and use your fingers to stretch and push the dough until it covers the tray, as thin as you can (it should be about 2cm thick) but with a slightly thicker edge. Then make small indents in the dough to make 'craters'.
5. Spread the surface of the dough with just enough tomato sauce to cover. Top with the tomato slices (if using) and the mozzarella. Season with some ground black pepper then bake for 25 minutes or until browned and/or cooked through. Top with basil and rocket.

For summer pizza (as in the picture)
Cook the pizza without cheese then tear the mozzarella over the pizza once it has come out of the oven. Sprinkle with the rocket and basil before slicing.

To make pizza snails
For another fun option, you can make pizza snails. Divide the dough mixture into four, then roll out on a floured surface until each looks like a long rectangle. Smother with tomato sauce (pesto is a lovely alternative), then top with ham or salami (optional) and finely shredded cheese – don't use the fresh tomatoes in this method as they are too big. Roll up each rectangle lengthways, like a very long sausage, then using a sharp knife cut the sausage into 5cm pieces. Transfer cut side up to a baking tray lined with baking paper, or to a non-stick tray, and bake for about 15–20 minutes or until the dough is cooked through.

KETCHUP

Of course there are bottled varieties that we all know and love, but a homemade sauce is more nutritious and less sweet, not to mention delicious. It's perfect as a pizza sauce or a tomato paste for bolognaise too. It is essential to use either a blender, stick blender or processor for this. Really ripe tomatoes are a lot sweeter, so you might need to adjust the quantity of sugar accordingly. If there are none in season then you can use Italian tinned tomatoes instead. It keeps in a bottle for up to a month in the fridge.

Makes 1.2 litres/or about 3–4 'ketchup' bottles

You will need

1 small carrot, peeled and cut into four
2 red onions, peeled and quartered
4 garlic cloves, peeled
2 tablespoons light olive oil or rapeseed oil
1kg mixed tomatoes (we use about 150g cherry tomatoes for sweetness, then make up the rest with big ripe tomatoes, core removed and cut into quarters)
3 heaped tablespoons tomato puree
4 tablespoons apple cider vinegar
3–4 tablespoons demerara sugar
1 tablespoon soy sauce
¼ teaspoon each ground ginger, cinnamon and allspice
A pinch of ground cloves
1½ teaspoons cornflour

Note: To sterilise bottles or jars, simmer in a large pan of boiling water for 5 minutes then carefully remove with tongs. Warning: the bottles will be extremely hot so ask an adult to help. Pour the ketchup into the bottles while they are still warm.

Preparation

1. In a food processor whizz the carrot, onion and garlic until chopped (or do by hand). Sauté over a gentle heat in a large pan with the oil until soft.

2. Add the tomatoes to the processor (no need to wash it first) and whizz until chopped (or you can chop by hand). Add to the pan with the remaining ingredients (only use 3 tablespoons of sugar to begin with), except the cornflour. Add ½ teaspoon sea salt flakes.

3. Bring up to the boil, then turn the heat down and simmer gently, partially covering with a lid, for 20–30 minutes, stirring every so often. The mixture should reduce to a thickish but still pourable sauce.

4. Mix the cornflour with a little cold water and add to the simmering sauce to cook for a further minute.

5. Leave to cool slightly then whizz in the processor or using a blender until completely smooth. Taste for seasoning/sweetness, adding more of anything needed. If it still has any pips remaining, strain the sauce through a sieve. Pour through a funnel into sterilised bottles or jars and seal closed with the lid.

MAGICAL CHOCOLATE FUDGE CAKE

You will need

225g good quality, dark chocolate chips
200g unsalted butter
4 eggs
175g golden caster sugar
2 teaspoons good quality vanilla extract
150g courgette, grated finely
100g raw peeled beetroot, grated finely
280g wholegrain stoneground spelt flour (or for a less wholemeal taste you can use 150g spelt with 130g plain flour)
1 teaspoon bicarbonate of soda
1 teaspoon baking powder

For the icing
75g dark chocolate chips
100g soft butter
200g icing sugar
1 teaspoon vanilla extract

To decorate
Chocolate sprinkles, raspberries and/or edible flower petals

Sometimes funny things happen in the kitchen. This started off as a brownie recipe but as if by magic it's turned into a delicious cake! The fact that it uses spelt flour, beetroot and courgette means loads of secret super nutrients and nobody will know! See if anyone can guess what the magical veggies are when they try the finished cake.

Makes about 20 squares

Preparation

1. Preheat the oven to 180°C/160°C fan/gas mark 4.
2. Melt 100g of chocolate chips with the butter in a bowl over simmering water or carefully in the microwave (if microwaving make sure you take it out before the chocolate has completely melted as it will continue to melt). Stir with a wooden spoon then cool for 5 minutes. Add the sugar, eggs, vanilla extract and the grated veggies and mix together.
3. Sieve over the flour, bicarbonate of soda and baking powder. Add any grainy bits left in the bottom of the sieve. Scrunch in ½ a level teaspoon of sea salt flakes, add the remaining chocolate chips and fold together.
4. Pour the cake mixture into a greased and baking paper-lined 20 x 25cm tray. Bake for 25 minutes until the cake is springy to touch. Remove from the tin and cool.
5. To make the icing, melt the chocolate and 1 tablespoon of water in a bowl again, as per method above. Leave to cool for 5 minutes, then add the butter, icing sugar and vanilla and whisk together until creamy.
6. Spread over the cooled cake and decorate with chocolate sprinkles, fresh raspberries and/or edible flower petals. Chill for 20 minutes before serving.

SNAIL SANDWICHES

No you don't have to eat snails! These pinwheel sandwiches are extremely cute and great fun for eating outside. You can change the filling to whatever you like best – peanut butter or ham also works well – just don't choose anything too chunky or you won't be able to roll them up.

Makes 6 pinwheels

You will need

2 slices bread
Softened butter
Marmite or Vegemite
2 teaspoons cream cheese, plus a little extra for assembling
3x5cm piece cucumber
2 chives, snipped into 3cm lengths
Cocktail sticks, to secure

Preparation

1. Flatten the bread using a rolling pin, rolling it out like you would pastry. Cut off the crusts.
2. Spread both slices of bread with a little butter, followed by some Marmite or Vegemite, then finish with cream cheese. Take one piece of bread and roll it tightly lengthways, pressing gently to seal at the outer edge. Repeat with the other piece of bread, and then cut both into 3x4cm pieces to make 6 pieces in total.
3. Cut the cucumber into quarters lengthways, and then cut off the seeds to create a flat slice.
4. Stick each snail pinwheel sandwich upright onto a cucumber base using a little extra cream cheese to help it hold. Using a cocktail stick, secure the front cucumber strip, tucking a couple of chives in either side. Serve the snails on logs or plates.

Orchard Fruit
Summer Berries
Rhubarb

You will need

25g water biscuits,
matzo, plain crackers or
breadcrumbs
1 large eating apple
½ onion, peeled
400g pork mince
1 large garlic clove, peeled
½ heaped teaspoon chopped
fresh sage, or 2 good pinches
dried sage
1 egg yolk
1½ teaspoons soy sauce
2 teaspoons oil, for frying

PORK & APPLE BURGERS

Juicy, tasty mini burgers are a real treat. I find that these are best when using crushed dry crackers instead of breadcrumbs, but both work. Rather than the mince you can also use top quality skinned sausages or sausage meat – just omit the crushed crackers (and the sage if using herby sausages). For more grown up flavours, feel free to add some chilli flakes, English mustard or paprika to the mixture. Anything goes!

Makes about 6 small burgers

Preparation

1. Put the crackers into a food bag and smash with a rolling pin until finely crushed.
2. Peel and core the apple, then grate along with the onion and garlic, quite finely onto a couple of pieces of kitchen paper. Scrunch the paper around the bits and squeeze to remove a little of their moisture.
3. In a bowl, using clean hands, mix the crackers, apple mixture, pork mince and all the other ingredients together. Add a good grinding black pepper and ½ teaspoon of sea salt flakes.
4. Form into 6 medium thickness mini burgers and chill for a minimum of 30 minutes.
5. Brush the burgers with oil and barbecue or grill for 4–6 minutes each side. Or you can heat the oil in a griddle pan and fry gently for 4–6 minutes each side or until brown and cooked through. Serve with mini burger buns (topped with some sliced tomato and crunchy lettuce if you like), veggie chips and kid-friendly slaw on page 102. A dollop of chutney, ketchup or barbecue sauce is also delicious on top.

How to build a campfire cooker

Building a real fire outdoors is great fun, but **safety is key** so always ask an adult to help you. You can build a fire directly on clear ground. Make a fire ring using stones or bricks and build up the sides to contain the ash. A grill rack can then be placed on top. Alternatively, a less messy solution is to find a fire proof container to hold your fire – such as an un-painted tin bath, metal fire pit dish or even a recycled deep foil tray or roasting tin. You can use secured chicken wire or a grill rack on top to cook your food. Old bricks or logs are ideal to use as a base underneath the container, to prevent the ground from being scorched. We used an old recycled tin bath, supported by a couple of bricks at each end.

Use a compact pile of dry leaves or screwed up paper to make a tinder to light. Twigs can be stacked in a criss-cross pattern or piled like a teepee on top. Carefully light the tinder (an adult must be present to help). Gradually add some kindling wood until the fire is burning well, then add small dry logs or charcoal. When the flames have subsided and the fire is hot, you are ready to cook.

CAMPFIRE SKEWERS

You will need

For the savoury skewers
4 long metal or wooden skewers
Large chunks of vegetables such as red pepper, courgette, cherry tomatoes, whole mushrooms, cooked baby new potatoes, cooked chunks of corn on the cob
Chunks of halloumi, chicken breast or pork sausage
2–3 tablespoons non-creamy salad dressing such as vinaigrette or balsamic

For the sweet skewers
4 long metal or wooden skewers
8 large marshmallows
Large chunks of fruit such as thick wedges of peach or nectarine, banana, pineapple or whole strawberries

There's nothing more fun than cooking your own lunch over an open fire. Just be careful. Fires are dangerous and this snack can get VERY hot and sticky! You can also cook these skewers over a barbecue. We've given recipes for savoury and sweet ones here.

Makes 4 sweet and 4 savoury skewers.

Preparation

1. Start by lighting your fire, following the instructions opposite.
2. If using wooden skewers then soak them in water for 30 mins (this prevents them from splintering and burning).
3. To make savoury skewers, mix your chosen ingredients with the salad dressing and some salt and pepper.
4. Thread the metal or wooden skewers with the chosen foods and leave covered in the fridge until you are ready to cook them.
5. Sweet skewers will take only a few minutes to cook and it's best to hold them a little way away from the grill to stop the marshmallows from melting too fast. Turn them as they cook. Savoury skewers will take longer and can be cooked directly on the grill or wire. Ask an adult to turn them carefully so that they don't burn. They should be nicely browned all over.

FRUITY YOGURT POTS

Pear, raspberry and orange zest
Rhubarb, apple and cinnamon
Plum, cherry and star anise
Apricot, nectarine and vanilla

A compote is what you get when fruit is cooked until it has collapsed. They are delicious on cereal, eaten warm with ice cream or custard or served with a spoonful of yogurt, as in this recipe. You can keep it chunkier or blend till smooth – that's up to you. Cooking the fruit does vary a bit timing wise as harder fruits will take longer to soften. The amount of sugar you add also depends on how sweet the fruit is, and how sweet you like it. So taste before adding too much. Chocolate drops sprinkled into the warm fruit is also another fun addition.

Makes 6–8 small pots or glasses

You will need

A couple of big handfuls (about 300g) raw fruit such as stoned sliced plums, peaches, nectarines or apricots, chopped rhubarb, halved de-stoned cherries, peeled, cored and sliced apple or pear or mixed berries
1–2 tablespoons apple or orange juice or water
½–2 tablespoons sugar or runny honey to sweeten
Greek or plain yogurt
Edible flowers or mint sprigs

Preparation

1. Put your chosen fruit combinations and flavours (see suggestions above left) into a pan with 1 tablespoon of juice or water. Cook the fruit gently, covered with a lid, for about 5–8 minutes, stirring every so often. If using a combination of hard and soft fruits e.g pears and raspberries or apples and apricots, then cook the harder fruit until softened, before adding the softer ones for the final few minutes.
2. Check to see how soft it is, sweeten to taste and add more liquid if needed. Once the fruit looks softened and 'collapsed', taste for sweetness, then cool. You can leave it as is, mash it with a potato masher or, for a really smooth one, blitz in a blender. Leave to cool.
3. Fill glasses or pots ¾ full with yogurt. Top with the fruit compote and a flower or mint sprig and chill until required.

TEN MINUTE JAM

Everyone needs a good jam in their life, and this one uses orange flower water to add a beautiful scent. You can thicken it using just chia seeds, rather than adding sugar (as below). However, having tried it out at home, we all decided that using just chia seeds makes it too pippy. So, this version has just enough sugar to preserve it, and some chia to thicken without giving you a mouthful of bits! Delicious spread on bread or toast or try it with some scones.

Makes 2 x 200g jars

You will need

500g raspberries, fresh or frozen
Juice of ½ lemon
200g sugar
1–2 teaspoons orange flower water or the zest of half an orange
2 heaped teaspoons chia seeds

Preparation

1. Put the raspberries (no need to defrost if using frozen), lemon juice and sugar into a large pan and stir over a medium heat to bring it slowly up to simmering point. When it begins to bubble, increase the heat and set your timer for 5 minutes. Let the jam really bubble away (you can stir it every so often) until it looks like it's starting to thicken.
2. Turn off the heat and stir in the orange flower water or zest and chia seeds.
3. Pour into sterilised jars, see page 150 (how to sterilise) and seal while still warm. Once cool, keep in the fridge for up to a month.

APPLE & BERRY CRUNCH

This is a very easy crumble, made by stirring melted butter into the dry ingredients to make a quick topping. You can add some chopped nuts, raisins or chocolate chips to the topping if you like. This recipe uses apples and berries but it is just as good made with plums, apricots or rhubarb. Cooking apples can also be used instead of eating apples but be sure to sprinkle over extra sugar as they are very tart.

Serves 4–6

You will need

For the crunch topping
180g plain flour or a mix of ½ plain and ½ spelt flour
125g sugar, ideally half white and half soft brown, though most sugars work
100g rolled oats
125g butter, melted

For the fruit
600g eating apples, peeled, cored and thinly sliced
300g berries such as raspberries, blackberries or tayberries
2 heaped tablespoons sugar
2 tablespoons orange juice or water

Preparation

1. Preheat the oven to 180°C/160°C fan/gas mark 4.
2. To make the topping, sieve the flour or flours into a bowl and stir in the sugar, oats and a pinch of salt. Using a knife, stir the mixture, while adding the melted butter in a slow drizzle. It should be clumpy but combined.
3. Put the apple slices and berries into a 1.2 litre baking dish, just big enough so that they reach about 2cm or so below the surface. Sprinkle over the sugar and add the juice.
4. Scatter over the crunch topping and pat down lightly.
5. Bake for 30–35 minutes or until the top is browned.

STRAWBERRY BUTTERFLY CAKES

As a child, Ghillie often made butterfly cakes using a similar vanilla cupcake recipe. The wings were made using slices of sponge dug out from the tops of the cake. This version is less fiddly and uses ripe strawberry slices and some colourful sprinkles instead.

Makes 12

You will need

175g soft butter
175g caster sugar
3 eggs
1½ teaspoon vanilla extract
175g self-raising flour

For the buttercream
150g soft butter
300g icing sugar
½ teaspoon vanilla extract
6 large strawberries and coloured sprinkles

Preparation

1. Preheat the oven to 180°C/160°C fan/gas mark 4. Put cupcake cases into a 12 hole cupcake tin.
2. In a large bowl, preferably using an electric whisk, beat together the soft butter and sugar until light and fluffy. Whisk in the eggs, one at a time, and then the vanilla. Sieve over the flour and using a large metal spoon, fold in, until completely mixed. Spoon about 2 heaped teaspoons of the mixture into each of the 12 cupcake cases. Bake for 12–15 minutes or until risen, golden brown and springy to the touch. Cool completely on a wire rack.
3. In another bowl put the butter for the icing and sieve over the icing sugar. Add the vanilla and whisk on a low speed until creamy. Pipe or spoon the mixture onto the centre of each cupcake.
4. Cut the strawberries into wing-like wedges, see photograph, and poke two into the icing on an angle, like a butterfly's wings. Decorate with sprinkles.

BLUEBERRY FLOWERPOT MUFFINS

These are Julia's family favourites. Using clay pots is not essential but it's a fun way to make them look a little like cute flower pots ready for planting. They are super easy to make and the crunchy 'soil' topping reminds Julia of her vegetable patch, where the blueberry bushes grow. You can use normal muffin cases, but if you use the pots, soak them in water for an hour before using, then grease the bottoms and line with baking paper.

Makes 12 muffins or 8–10 clay pots

You will need

200g spelt or plain flour
½ heaped teaspoon bicarbonate of soda
1 heaped teaspoon baking powder
150g caster sugar
60g butter, melted
1 large lemon, zest and juice
120ml milk
1 large egg
150g blueberries

For the crumble topping (this makes double)
120g spelt or plain flour
65g rolled oats
75g soft light brown sugar
75g butter

Preparation

The crumble topping makes double the amount you need and it freezes beautifully in a tub. This can be a great time saver for the next time you bake these delicious muffins, but feel free to halve the amounts if you prefer to make just enough for one batch..

1. Preheat the oven to 200°C/180°C fan/gas mark 6. First of all make the crumble topping. Mix the flour, oats and sugar with a pinch of salt and add the butter, cut into small pieces. Using your fingers, rub the butter into the flour and oat mixture until it resembles fine breadcrumbs. Set to one side.
2. Mix all the dry ingredients for the muffins together in a bowl, with a pinch of salt.
3. In a jug, and using a fork, mix the butter, lemon juice and zest, milk and egg. Pour it over the dry ingredients and fold together as lightly as you can, adding the blueberries towards the end.
4. Fill a muffin tray with paper cases then divide the mixture between them (or spoon into soaked, lined clay pots if using).
5. Sprinkle with half of the crumble topping.
6. Bake for 20–25 minutes or until golden then cool.

ETON MESS
ICE CREAM CAKE

Meringues, strawberries and cream – what a combo! Even though
this is really a cheat's recipe the end result is a show stopper – great
for a party or to end a special meal.

Makes one loaf to serve 6

You will need

250ml fresh double cream
1 tablespoon vanilla extract or 1 vanilla pod, seeds scraped
250g fresh custard, ideally a good quality shop bought carton
250g fresh raspberries, or frozen defrosted raspberries
3 large meringues (shop bought is fine)
225g ripe strawberries, hulled (green tops cut off)
1–2 tablespoons icing sugar (optional)

Preparation

1. Line a standard 900g loaf tin with non PVC cling film or reusable food wrap, letting
    about 7–8cm hang over the edges. This makes it easier to turn out the loaf.
2. In a large bowl, beat the cream and vanilla with an electric whisk until it is has formed
    soft peaks which stand up on their own. With the whisk on low speed, slowly pour in the
    custard and keep mixing until combined.
3. In a bowl, use a fork to mash the raspberries, so that they are just a little broken down.
4. Add the raspberries to the cream and fold in using a spatula. Then add the meringues,
    crushing between your fingers as you put them into the bowl. Fold in.
5. Slice 2 strawberries, and place the pieces around the edges of the inside of the tin. They
    will look very pretty once the loaf comes out. Spoon the mixture into the tin and smooth
    the top. Wrap the cling film or reusable food wrap over the top and then freeze for 3–4
    hours until firm.
6. In the meantime, blend the remaining strawberries (add 1–2 tablespoons icing sugar if
    not sweet enough) to make a sauce. When ready to serve, remove loaf from the freezer
    about 10 minutes before you want to eat it. It will need to defrost slightly before you slice
    it. Unwrap it and carefully place a plate on top. Turn it over so that the loaf is sitting on
    the plate, and slide off the tin. Serve the sauce in a jug or pour a little over the loaf before
    slicing.

MESSY TART

This free-form tart works with all sorts of seasonal fruit combinations: peach, pear or plum slices, raspberries, stoned cherries or, as below, rhubarb, strawberries and blueberries. Pretty much anything goes, so either mix it up to your liking or stick to just one fruit. Just remember that some fruits take longer to cook than others, so adjust the size of the pieces accordingly – raw apple will take longer to soften than raspberries, so the apples should be thinly sliced. It's best to assemble the tart right before baking to prevent a soggy bottom. However, you could make and even roll out the pastry and prepare the fruit earlier in the day.

Serves 6

You will need

For the pastry
180g plain flour or a mix of half spelt and half plain flour
1 tablespoon caster sugar
120g cold butter, cubed
110g full fat cream cheese
2 tablespoons iced water

For the filling
200g rhubarb, cut into inch-long pieces
275g strawberries, leafy tops removed, and halved
100g blueberries
1 tablespoon cornflour (or 2 level teaspoons for non-juicy fruits such as rhubarb, stone or orchard fruits)
1 teaspoon vanilla extract, or the scraped seeds from half a vanilla pod
2 tablespoons sugar
2 tablespoons ground almonds
1 heaped tablespoon flaked almonds
1 small egg, beaten

Preparation

1. Put the flour, sugar and a pinch of salt into a food processor and whizz for 5 seconds. Add the butter and spoonfuls of cream cheese.
2. Pulse for 10 seconds or until it looks like crumbs. Add the water and pulse until it forms a dough. Pour onto a large piece of non PVC cling film and press into a ball. Wrap and freeze for 15 minutes to chill it quickly.
3. Preheat the oven to 200°C/180°C fan/gas mark 6.
4. Mix together the fruit, cornflour and vanilla and set aside.
5. Put a large piece of baking paper onto the work surface, then sprinkle with the flour. Unwrap the pastry and put into the centre of paper. Sprinkle a little flour over the pastry and roll out to a large thin circle 5–7mm thick. Move the pastry and its paper onto a flat baking tray. Spoon the ground almonds onto the pastry and spread out until about 5cm from the edge. Heap the fruit on top of the almonds.
6. With the aid of the baking paper, pull up the sides of the pastry to hug the fruit and stop it falling out. Don't worry if the pastry has to fold over itself. Brush the pastry with beaten egg then stick the flaked almonds to it, patting them on with your fingers.
7. Bake for about 40 minutes or until the pastry is brown and cooked all the way through. Serve hot with vanilla ice cream or custard.

WEEKE

ND FUN!

YOU WILL NEED

For the pots:
Old newspaper
Small tin can, empty water bottle
or similar item
Some masking tape
(or use toilet roll tubes)
For planting
Flower or herb seeds
Tray
Multi-purpose compost
Bigger pots to transfer plants
Wooden lolly sticks and pen
Trowel or small spade
Water sprayer (use an old
cleaning spray bottle, once
washed out)

Little Grower's Tip

Not all plants are edible!
In fact some can be very
poisonous, so always
double check before
picking and tasting any
flowers or plants.

Little Grower's Tip

Sunflowers grow best in
a deep pot or directly in
the ground. The deeper
the pot the taller they will
grow. Bury a stick or cane
in the soil to tie to the
plant as it grows so it won't
fall over. Don't forget to
collect the seeds once the
plant has died – they are
delicious and the birds
also love to eat them.

LITTLE POTS OF SUNSHINE

Plant some flower seeds in homemade pots

Do you fancy measuring yourself against a sunflower or brightening up a windowsill with colourful flowers? Homemade pots are easy to make and can be planted into soil once the plants are bigger. Old toilet roll tubes make brilliant seed-sowing pots too. Many varieties of flower seeds are sold in garden centres. Some flowers can be eaten as well, such as violets, pansies, marigolds, nasturtiums, violas, lavender, cornflowers, borage, roses, fruit blossoms and herb flowers. Add edible flowers to salads or decorate cakes or biscuits with them (see pages 112 & 128). Spring is a great season to sow seeds. You can start them off 6–8 weeks ahead if you like, in a bright, sunny spot indoors.

1. To make plant pots, cut strips of newspaper 4 pages thick, to the same width as the can or bottle. Place the can or bottle on its side at the end of one of the strips, leaving enough free at the end to fold in and cover the base. Roll each sheet tightly around the can or bottle, folding in as you go. Repeat four times, each time rolling the other way. Secure with some tape and slide out the can or bottle.
2. Put your little pots or toilet rolls onto a tray and fill ¾ full with compost.
3. If you are growing sunflowers then poke one seed into the soil in each pot. With other varieties, a few seeds should be scattered evenly over the soil.
4. Top with more compost to just below the surface, then give them a good water. A spray bottle is good for this, as ideally you don't want to drench your newspaper too much. Pop in a named lolly stick.
5. Keep the compost moist by watering every day and you will soon see green shoots appearing.
6. When the plants are 5–6cm tall you will need to carefully transplant the plant and its pot to a bigger pot filled with compost. Just make a hole to fit the pot in, then cover with more soil and give it a water. As the plants grow, buds and then flowers will appear.

Weekend Fun Activity

YOU WILL NEED

2 oranges
2 lemons
Serrated knife
Spoon
Skewer
Garden twine or string
Scissors
250g lard (a type of fat)
About 10 tbsp wild bird seed
Bowl

FEED THE BIRDS

Make your own seed feeders

Whether you live in a town or the country, there are birds everywhere. As well as being wonderful to look at and listen to, they are an important part of many ecosystems – pollinating flowers and dispersing seeds amongst other things.

Giving birds a little extra food in the winter and early spring when it's cold outside and the trees are bare is a wonderful way to help them survive. Hanging a feeder will attract birds to your garden, patio or balcony so you can enjoy watching them. Wild birds will always be timid at first, but as long as you stay still and quiet they will come and feed near you eventually. See how many different types you can spot and, if you like, you can draw them in a notebook then look up their names.

1. Carefully cut each fruit in half. Then cut a very thin slice from the round bottom of each half so that the fruit can sit upright (but without making a hole through the flesh).
2. Using a spoon, scoop out the insides from the fruit (you can eat the fruit or use the juice to add to the lemonade on page 123. Oranges will bring delicious flavour to the lemonade).
3. Using a skewer, make two tiny holes in the skin on each side at the top of the fruit. Take one long piece of garden twine or string and feed each end evenly through the holes, then knot to make a cradle. Sit the hollowed fruit in a dish.
4. Melt the lard a little if its chilled and hard, then mix with enough bird seed to make a seedy cake mix. Spoon the mixture into the fruit halves and pat down tightly.
5. Chill until cold then hang on a branch or post.

Please note: these are great for birds to eat when it is cold outside. However you should remove them once the weather warms up as melted fat isn't so good for our feathery friends.

Weekender's Tip

Small empty yogurt pots can be used instead of fruit halves if you like. Simply make a hole at the base and feed through some string. Tie in a big knot, pulling some extra string through, then fill with the seed mix, pressing down to make it firm. Once chilled, remove the plastic pot using some scissors and hang the seed cake upside down.

YOU WILL NEED

Handful of scented flower
petals and herb leaves such as
lavender, rose, spearmint,
jasmine or basil
Orange rind, cinnamon sticks,
vanilla pods or lemongrass can
also be added if you like
Distilled water
Saucepan
Heatproof bowl to sit snugly
over the pan
Jar or spray bottle

MAGICAL FLOWER POTIONS

Create your own flower-scented water

Pick some edible flower petals and transform them into a magical perfume that you can spray on your pillow, add to your bath water or use for making spells! Scented, edible flower water can also be used in recipes.

You can easily make a bottle or jar of scented flower and herb water just by heating leaves and petals in water. Pretend you are a real perfume maker, and test different combinations of flowers and herbs until you have found your perfect scent! Keep the freshly made water in a jar or spray bottle. You should always use scented petals that haven't been sprayed with pesticides and chemicals, so it's best to use ones you have grown or that have been grown organically. Ask an adult to help you choose which flowers you are allowed to use and ask them to help you when heating them too. Choosing colourful petals will also turn the water a lovely colour!

1. Put the flower petals, herbs, leaves and any other additional scented infusions together into the heatproof bowl.
2. Cover with enough water to submerge the flowers but not too much that they will be too diluted. A cm or two above the flowers is about right.
3. Ask an adult to help with the next part. Half fill the pan with hot water and place the bowl on top.
4. Heat the pan over a medium flame until the water in the bowl begins to simmer. Keep heating gently so the water picks up the scents and colours from the flowers. Once the flowers have lost their colour, allow to cool then strain the water through a sieve into a jar or bottle.
5. Keep in the fridge for 2–3 weeks. Always check it's fresh before spraying.

Weekend Fun Activity

YOU WILL NEED

1 ripe tomato
Serrated knife
Recycled and washed plastic fruit punnet and lid
Fine multi-purpose or potting compost
Wooden lolly sticks
Pen or pencil
Small tray
Water sprayer (use an old cleaning spray bottle, once washed out)
Small chopping board

Little Grower's Tip

Don't dampen the compost before you place the tomato slices on top. Tomatoes contain enough moisture to help the seeds germinate. Too much water and they will rot.

Little Grower's Tip

Don't throw away the root ends of leeks or spring onions when they are chopped off in the kitchen. You can replant them and they will grow again. Make sure that all the roots are underground and the stem is poking about 1cm above the soil. In a few days you will notice new shoots appearing.

PLANT YOUR OWN PACKED LUNCH!

Make a mini greenhouse

We all know how important it is to try to save our planet and you can help in lots of ways. Next time you go to the shops, if you can't avoid buying plastic, you can save the plastic fruit punnets, such as the ones that strawberries and other fruits are sold in. Reuse them by turning them into mini greenhouses. The lids help keep the soil warm, creating a happy place for seeds, such as tomatoes, to grow big and strong. They are the perfect size to sit on an indoor windowsill; you don't even have to take the lid off to watch your seedlings at work! They already have holes in the bottom for drainage, so make sure you sit them on a tray to protect the paintwork.

1. Fill the punnet with multi-purpose compost.
2. Tap the punnet a few times to remove any air pockets and rub any lumps with your hands. Then top it up and pat the compost to make it flat.
3. Cut the ripe tomato on a board into 2 slices about ½ cm thick – you can eat the rest. Place the slices carefully on top of the compost, keeping as many of the seeds intact as you can.
4. Spray the inside of the lid of the fruit punnet lightly with water, and place on top. If the weather is warm and/or humid it is a good idea to cover the tomato slices with an extra, thin layer of compost
5. Move the mini greenhouse to a warm, sunny place inside, like a windowsill. Place it on a small tray to catch water spills.
6. In about 10 days when the seedlings appear, remove the lid and discard, then spray the compost with more water when it looks dry. The tomato will decompose so don't worry if it looks mouldy or dry.
7. Soon the seedlings will grow bigger and look like tiny trees with 2 leaves at the top, this is the time to move them to bigger pots to continue to grow. Now you can follow the instructions on page 38 under 'transplanting' to continue growing your tomatoes.
8. Put in a named wooden lolly stick to remember what you have planted.

Weekender's Tip

Have fun trying to plant seeds from other fruit and veggies in your packed lunch. Lemons, peppers, pumpkins, pomegranates and chillies can also be grown from seed. It's often best to dry them out on a sheet of kitchen paper in a warm place before planting.

Save The Planet Tip

It's a good idea to set your worms free in the garden after about a week.

YOU WILL NEED

Old plastic one litre bottle
Wet sand
Damp soil
Veggie peelings
Worms
Dark paper or card
Scissors

A CAFÉ FOR WORMS

Design your very own wormery

Worms live underground in every garden. They help to increase the amount of air and water in the soil, making it a healthier place for plants to grow. Worms break down leaves and grass into food that plants can use. When worms eat, they leave behind 'castings' that are a very valuable type of fertilizer. You can collect some by making your own wormery – which is like a restaurant for worms! It will be full of veggie peelings so the worms can take their pick – maybe carrot for breakfast, potato for lunch and some sprouts for supper. You can often find worms under stones, in damp places and of course underground. Get a trowel or use your hands to dig some up. If you haven't got a garden to dig in, then – believe it or not – you can also buy worms online!

1. Using some scissors, cut ⅓ from the top of your plastic bottle and stand the bottle up. Make two or three holes in the top section.
2. Make layers of wet sand and soil – about 4cm of each until you reach ¾ way up the bottle, it will look stripey.
3. Add a big handful of delicious veggie peelings.
4. Add some worms, two or three will do. Then slide on the top section to prevent the worms from escaping.
5. Keep the bottle dark by covering with some dark paper or card, secured with some tape or paper clips. Just remove it when you want to study your squiggly friends.
6. Make the worms happy by keeping the soil damp with a sprinkling of water, and adding extra food peelings.
7. Always wash your hands when you've been handling the wormery, and especially the worms themselves!
8. You can name your worms if you like – the longer the name, the longer the worm?!

YOU WILL NEED

Old jam jars (no lids needed)
Potting or multi-purpose
compost
Spoonful of gravel or fine stones
Small potted herb plants
such as basil, mint, rosemary,
sage, oregano or thyme
Spoon
Label and pen
Some pretty string or ribbon
Scissors
Chalk paint and brush if you
plan to paint your jars

A PRESENT FROM THE GARDEN

Herb filled jam jars for someone special

Everybody loves receiving a homemade gift, especially one they can use! These pretty jars of herbs are the perfect present for a teacher, mum, dad or grandparent. Using recycled jars makes them inexpensive too. They will keep for weeks, if regularly watered, and can sit on a table or a windowsill, ready to use in recipes. You could make just one, or put a collection together in a decorated shoe box or small wooden crate. Jars also look pretty when painted with chalk paints, if you have some.

You can buy small herb plants cheaply from school fairs or farmers' markets. Your local garden centre will also stock them.

1. If you are planning to paint your jars then do so first, to allow the paint to dry completely.
2. First put 2cm or so of gravel in the bottom of the jar. This will help with drainage.
3. Fill your jars to the top with potting or multi-purpose compost and tap to remove any air holes. Pat down a little and add a bit more soil so that it reaches just under the rim.
4. Using a spoon or your fingers, part the soil to make a well in the compost and pour in a little water to dampen.
5. Carefully remove your herb plant from its pot and snuggle into the hole.
6. Pat the soil in around the herb, adding a little more if needed. Give the jar a water then clean around the rim, where some of the soil and water might have escaped.
7. Make a label with the herb's name on one side and who the present is for on the other side. Attach it to the jar using string or ribbon.
8. Tie more ribbon or string around the top in a bow. Make sure to keep the soil inside your jar damp at all times.

YOU WILL NEED

Shallow bowl, old bird bath, sweetie tin or recycled plastic container

Something to stand the container on – an old garden table or stool

2-3 handfuls of sand and handful of manure, optional

Small rocks or stones

Water (with a little sugar added for a sweeter treat)

Overripe fruits such as bananas, oranges, apples, pears and strawberries

Serrated knife

Save The Planet Tip

Don't throw away your overripe fruit, feed it to the butterflies!

HOST A BUTTERFLY BANQUET

Feed your fluttery friends their favourite foods

Although butterflies live all over the world, sadly numbers are declining. So it's important that we do our bit to make caterpillars and butterflies feel welcome, with lots of food to eat! Caterpillars feed on leaves and flower buds, butterflies on nectar. Look online to find out which butterflies live in your local area and which plants those caterpillars and butterflies like to eat. You could plant some butterfly-friendly flowers in the garden, in pots or in a window box.

This butterfly banquet provides our fluttery friends with a sugary snack to give them energy. Butterflies love fruits such as overripe bananas and oranges – especially when they have gone a bit soggy and mushy. A pool of shallow water acts as a valuable drinking station, and if you add some stones they can perch on them to enjoy the sunshine.

1. Position your container on a table or stool outside in a sunny place. Put a layer of sand, manure if you have some (butterflies love this!) and some small rocks or stones in the base of your container. Add about 3–4cm water (or water mixed with sugar).
2. Cut up your fruit, leaving the peel on, and add it to your butterfly garden. Overripe fruit is best for butterflies.
3. Watch your butterfly garden from a distance and see who comes to visit.

Save The Planet Tip

Try to avoid using
pesticides in the garden
as these are harmful to
bees, butterflies and other
insects.

YOU WILL NEED

Old tin can, broken flower pot or
old plastic bottle cut in half
Dry sticks
Garden canes
Feathers
Pine cones
Leaves
Bark
Hollow stalks like bamboo
(bugs love these)

Weekender's Fact

Did you know your
garden could host more
than 2000 species of
visiting minibeasts?

BUILD A BUG HOTEL

Construct a minibeast mansion

Spiders, centipedes, millipedes, ladybirds, woodlice and other insects are important to nature. As well as being part of the food chain, they help to pollinate plants, to decompose and eat dead and decaying matter and to recycle nutrients back into the soil. You can help them by building a bug hotel. It can start as one bedroom for your little friends and finish up as a massive luxury resort! You can keep making more and adding them, either in amongst some logs or piled up between wooden pallets, held up by bricks. You could also tie some string around your hotel and hang it up.

Just make sure you ask an adult where is the best place for your minibeast mansion, so it doesn't get in the way. Bugs and beasties love to hang out in cool, dark nooks and crannies!

1. Choose a container for your bug hotel.
2. Break up sticks and stalks so that they can fit inside, without sharp ends poking out too much.
3. Stuff your container with a mix of sticks, canes, pine cones, leaves, feathers and bark.
4. Find a quiet, dark location to keep your bug hotel, ideally sheltered. If you like you can fill in around the edges with logs, bricks, stones, tiles, bark and straw.
5. Have a look under logs and rocks and see if you can find some bugs to introduce to your hotel.
6. Make a welcome sign, so your bugs know you are open for business!

YOU WILL NEED

Fruit, veg, herb and flower seeds
Small envelopes
Coloured pencils or chalks
Pen
Box for storing
(such as a shoe box)

STORE YOUR SEEDS FROM A-Z

Design your own seed library

Make your very own seed library for leftover or foraged fruit and vegetable seeds, using small envelopes and some colouring chalks or pencils. Once you have decorated the front, you can write all sorts of useful information on the back, using what you have learnt from this book and from instructions on the back of bought seed packets. Include the date you collected them, as seeds have a life of 4–5 years. After that they won't grow.

You can store them in a decorated small box, old tin or plastic container. Keep in a cool dry place until ready to use.

Little Grower's Tip

Make sure your seeds are completely dry before you store them.

1. Use one envelope for each type of seed variety, for example one for peas, one for radishes and one for carrots. If you are using different varieties of the same plant then use separate envelopes for those, as they might have different planting times and conditions.
2. Using chalks or pencils, decorate your envelopes with pictures of the fruit and vegetables.
3. On the back of the envelope write any useful information – name and variety, best month to grow, watering instructions etc.
4. Choose a box big enough to hold the seed packets neatly. You can decorate this too, if you like.
5. Seal your envelopes to stop moisture from getting in and ruining your seeds. Store in a cool dry place.

Index ▪ cooking ▪ growing ▪ activities

Apples
Apple and Berry Crunch 167
Crunchy, Fruity Slaw 102
Fruity Yogurt Pots 162
Gardener's Cake 112
Host a Butterfly Banquet 192
Pork and Apple Burgers 158
Rainbow Rolls 124
Apple and Berry Crunch 167
Apricots
Fruity Yogurt Pots 162
Asparagus
Easy-Peasy Garden Salad 119
Avocado
Green Dip 101
Rainbow Rolls 124
Bacon
Squeaky Salad 120
Ten Veg Soup 140
Bagels
Broccoli Trees with Garlic Crumbs 132
Banana
Campfire Skewers 161
Host a Butterfly Banquet 192
Basil 28, 29
A Present From the Garden 191
How to grow 28
Magical Flower Potions 185
Pesto Pasta Salad 138
Shopping for Herbs 28
Ten Veg Soup 140
Terrific Tray Bake Pizza 146
The Best Pesto for Kids 127
Beans
Green Dip 101
How to grow 52
Pesto Pasta Salad 138
Runner 52
Sausage and Veggie Sleepover 108
Bees 18, 19, 193
Beetroot
Beets the Washing Up 62
How to grow 64
Magical Chocolate Fudge Cake 153
Pink Dip 98
Beets the Washing Up 62
Biodegradable Pots 14, 15, 80, 181
Birds 18, 182
Feed the Birds 182
Biscuits
Cheese and Rosemary Shortbreads 129
Flower Petal Shortbreads 128
Blackberries
Apple and Berry Crunch 167
Blueberries
Blueberry Flowerpot Muffins 170
Here We Go Round The Blueberry Bush 88
How to grow 90
Messy Tart 174
Brassicas
Broccoli Trees with Garlic Crumbs 132
Kale Crisps 133
Sticky Salmon 134

Ten Veg Soup 140
Bread and Breadcrumbs
Broccoli Trees with Garlic Crumbs 132
Easy-Peasy Garden Salad 119
Snail Sandwiches 154
Broad Beans
Green Dip 101
Broccoli
Broccoli Trees with Garlic Crumbs 132
Eat Your Greens! 75
How to grow 76
Sticky Salmon 134
Bucket and Spade Veggies 24
Bugs 18, 195
Build a Bug Hotel 195
Burger
Pork and Apple Burgers 158
Butterflies 18, 169, 192
Host a Butterfly Banquet 192
Strawberry Butterfly Cakes 169
Butterfly Banquet 192
Butternut Squash
How to grow 50
Orange Dip 100
Pumpkin and Courgette Fritters 145
Cabbage
Crunchy, Fruity Slaw 102
Ten Veg Soup 140
Café for Worms 189
Cakes
Blueberry Flowerpot Muffins 170
Eton Mess Ice Cream Cake 173
Gardener's Cake 112
Magical Chocolate Fudge Cake 153
Strawberry Butterfly Cakes 169
Campfire
Making 160
Campfire Skewers 161
Campfire Skewers 161
Can of Tomatoes 37
Carrots
Bucket and Spade Veggies 24
Cheesy Root Veg Bake 111
Gardener's Cake 112
How to grow 26
Ketchup 150
Orange Dip 100
Mini but Mighty Veggie Bites 104
Rainbow Rolls 124
Ten Veg Soup 140
Veggie Fries 96
Caterpillars 18, 192
Celery
Crunchy, Fruity Slaw 102
Ten Veg Soup 140
Chard
Eat Your Greens! 75
How to grow 76
Cheese
Campfire Skewers 161
Cheese and Rosemary Shortbreads 129
Cheesy Root Veg Bake 111
Hedgehog Potatoes 107

Mini but Mighty Veggie Bites 104
Orange Dip 100
Pesto Pasta Salad 138
Pumpkin, Feta and Courgette Fritters 145
Squeaky Salad 120
Ten Veg Soup 140
Terrific Tray Bake Pizza 146
The Best Pesto for Kids 127
Cheesy Root Veg Bake 111
Cherries
Fruity Yogurt Pots 162
Cherry Tomatoes
Campfire Skewers 161
Ketchup 150
Pesto Pasta Salad 138
Sausage and Veggie Sleepover 108
Chicken
Campfire Skewers 161
Rainbow Rolls 124
Squiggly Noodle Soup 137
Chickpeas
Orange Dip 100
Chilli
Broccoli Trees with Garlic Crumbs 132
Rainbow Rolls 124
Chips 96
Chitting 41
Chives
A Present From the Garden 191
Easy-Peasy Garden Salad 119
How to grow 30
Pesto Pasta Salad 138
Shopping for Herbs 28
Snail Sandwiches 154
Chocolate
Fruity Yogurt Pots 162
Magical Chocolate Fudge Cake 153
Colander 44
Coleslaw
Crunchy, Fruity Slaw 102
Compost
Bought 13
How to make 12, 13
Leaf 13
Multi-purpose 13
Potting 13
Coriander
A Present From the Garden 192
Rainbow Rolls 124
How to grow 30
Shopping for Herbs 28
Squiggly Noodle Soup 137
Courgettes
Campfire Skewers 161
How to grow 50
Magical Chocolate Fudge Cake 153
Pumpkin and Courgette Fritters 145
Squash in a Tub 49
Ten Veg Soup 140
Crate 75
Cress
Egg Friends 80
How to grow 82

Crisps, Pitta **101**
Crumble
    Apple and Berry Crunch 167
    Blueberry Flowerpot Muffins 170
Crunch, Apple and Berry **167**
Crunchy, Fruity Slaw 102
Cucumber
    Pesto Pasta Salad 138
    Rainbow Rolls 124
    Snail Sandwiches 154
Cupcakes
    Strawberry Butterfly Cakes 169
Desserts and Puddings
    Apple and Berry Crunch 167
    Eton Mess Ice Cream Cake 173
    Fruity Yogurt Pots 162
    Messy Tart 174
Dips
    Green Dip 101
    Orange Dip 100
    Pink Dip 98
Dill
    Cheese and Rosemary Shortbreads 129
    Pumpkin and Courgette Fritters 145
Drinks
    Mint and Raspberry Lemonade 123
Earthing Up
    Leeks 34
    Potatoes 41
Easy-Peasy Garden Salad 119
Eat Your Greens! 75
Eco-pots 15
Edible Flowers 85
    Easy-Peasy Garden Salad 119
    Flower Petal Shortbreads 128
    Fruity Yogurt Pots 162
    Gardener's Cake 112
    Little Pots of Sunshine 181
    Magical Chocolate Cake 153
    Magical Flower Potions 185
    Pesto Pasta Salad 138
Egg Friends 80
Egg Shells 15, 16, 80
Eton Mess Ice Cream Cake 173
Feed the Birds 182
Fish
    See individual
Flower Petal Shortbreads 128
Flowerpot Muffins 170
Flowers 16, 18-19, 85
    Flower Petal Shortbreads 128
    Fruity Yogurt Pots 162
    Gardener's Cake 112
    How to grow 181
    Little Pots of Sunshine 181
    Magical Chocolate Fudge Cake 153
    Pesto Pasta Salad 138
Fork, garden **10**
Fries 96
Fritters
    Pumpkin and Courgette Fritters 145
Fruits
    See individual

Fruity Yogurt Pots 162
Garden Salad 119
Gardener's Cake 112
Gardening Basics 10
Garlic
    Broccoli Trees with Garlic Crumbs 132
    Cheesy Root Veg Bake 111
    How to grow 85
    Ketchup 150
    Orange Dip 100
    Mini but Mighty Veggie Bites 104
    Pork and Apple Burgers 158
    Pumpkin and Courgette Fritters 145
    Rainbow Rolls 124
    Sausage and Veggie Sleepover 108
    Smelly Feet 85
    Squiggly Noodle Soup 137
    Sticky Salmon 134
    Ten Veg Soup 140
    The Best Pesto for Kids 127
Ginger
    Rainbow Rolls 124
    Squiggly Noodle Soup 137
    Sticky Salmon 134
Greens
    Eat Your Greens! 75
    How to grow 76
    Pesto Pasta Salad 138
    Squiggly Noodle Soup 137
Green Beans
    Pesto Pasta Salad 138
    Sausage and Veggie Sleepover 108
Greenhouse, Make a Mini **186**
Green Dip 101
Ham
    Terrific Tray Bake Pizza 146
Hanging Basket 57
Hardening Off
    Squashes 50
Harvesting Chart 20
Hedgehog Potatoes 107
Herbs
    See individual herb names
    A Present From the Garden 191
    How to grow 30
    Magical Flower Potions 185
    Shopping for Herbs 28
Here We Go Round The Blueberry Bush 88
Hessian
    Bag 28
    Crate lining 75
    Hanging basket lining 57
    Sack 40
Host a Butterfly Banquet 192
How to Grow
    See individual gardening projects
Ice Cream Cake, Eton Mess **173**
Insects 18, 193
    Build a Bug Hotel 195
Jam
    Ten Minute Jam 165
Kale
    Eat Your Greens! 75

    How to grow 76
    Kale Crisps 133
    Ten Veg Soup 140
Kale Crisps 133
Kebabs
    Campfire Skewers 161
Ketchup 150
Know Your Onions 70
Leeks
    How to grow 34
    Mini but Mighty Veggie Bites 104
    Plant Your Own Packed Lunch 186
    We've Sprung a Leek! 32
Lemonade
    Mint and Raspberry Lemonade 123
Lemongrass
    Squiggly Noodle Soup 137
Lemons
    Blueberry Flowerpot Muffins 170
    Broccoli Trees with Garlic Crumbs 132
    Easy-Peasy Garden Salad 119
    Flower Petal Shortbreads 128
    Mint and Raspberry Lemonade 123
    Pesto Pasta Salad 138
    Squeaky Salad 120
    Sticky Salmon 134
    Ten Minute Jam 165
    The Best Pesto for Kids 127
Lettuce
    Easy Peasy Garden Salad 119
    How to grow 46
    Rainbow Rolls 124
    Squeaky Salad 120
    Winter, how to grow 47
Little Pots of Sunshine 181
Magical Chocolate Fudge Cake 153
Magical Flower Potions 185
Make a Tee 'Pea' 53
Make Your Own Pots 16, 15, 181
Mangetout
    How to grow 54
Marjoram
    A Present From the Garden 191
    Shopping for Herbs 28
    How to grow 30
Marshmallow
    Campfire Skewers 161
Meringues
    Eton Mess Ice Cream Cake 173
Messy Tart 174
Mini but Mighty Veggie Bites 104
Mint
    A Present From the Garden 191
    Flower Petal Shortbreads 128
    Fruity Yogurt Pots 162
    How to grow 30
    Mint and Raspberry Lemonade 123
    Rainbow Rolls 124
    Shopping for Herbs 28
Mint and Raspberry Lemonade 123
Muffins
    Blueberry Flowerpot Muffins 170
Mulch, Leaf **13**

Mushrooms
Campfire Skewers 161
Natural Pesticide 16
Nectarines
Campfire Skewers 161
Fruity Yogurt Pots 162
Squeaky Salad 120
New Potatoes
see potatoes
Nitrogen Feed 86, 90
How to make 64
Noodles
Rainbow Rolls 124
Squiggly Noodle Soup 137
Onions
Cheesy Root Veg Bake 111
How to grow 72
Ketchup 150
Know Your Onions 70
Pork and Apple Burgers 158
Sausage and Veggie Sleepover 108
Sets 70
Spring, Green Dip 101
Spring, Squiggly Noodle Soup 137
Spring, Pumpkin and Courgette Fritters 145
Ten Veg Soup 140
Oranges
Apple and Berry Crunch 167
Gardener's Cake 112
Host a Butterfly Banquet 192
Ten Minute Jam 165
Sticky Salmon 134
Orange Dip 100
Orange Flower
Ten Minute Jam 165
Orchard Fruits
Apple and Berry Crunch 167
Crunchy, Fruity Slaw 102
Fruity Yogurt Pots 162
Gardener's Cake 112
Pork and Apple Burgers 158
Oregano
A Present From the Garden 191
How to grow 30
Shopping for Herbs 28
Ten Veg Soup 140
Terrific Tray Bake Pizza 146
Orzo Pasta
Pesto Pasta Salad 138
Pears
Fruity Yogurt Pots 162
Host a Butterfly Banquet 192
Pak Choi
Eat Your Greens! 75
How to grow 76
Squiggly Noodle Soup 137
Parsley
A Present From the Garden 191
Cheese and Rosemary Shortbreads 129
How to grow 30
Sausage and Veggie Sleepover 108
Shopping for Herbs 28

Parsnips
Bucket and Spade Veggies 24
Cheesy Root Veg Bake 111
Gardener's Cake 112
How to grow 26
Veggie Fries 96
Pasta
Pesto Pasta Salad 138
Ten Veg Soup 140
Peaches
Campfire Skewers 161
Fruity Yogurt Pots 162
Peas
Green Dip 101
How to grow 54
Easy Peasy Garden Salad 119
Make a Tee 'Pea' 53
Pea Shoots
Easy-Peasy Garden Salad 119
How to grow 68
Sweetie Peas 67
Peppers
Campfire Skewers 161
Orange Dip 100
Rainbow Rolls 124
Sausage and Veggie Sleepover 108
Pesticide 189
Natural 16
Pesto
Pesto Pasta Salad 138
The Best Pesto for Kids 127
Pesto Pasta Salad 138
Pick 'n' Mix Lettuce 44
Pineapple
Campfire Skewers 161
Pink Dip 101
Pitta Crisps 101
Pizza
Pizza Snails 149
Terrific Tray Bake Pizza 146
Pizza Snails 149
Plant Your Packed Lunch! 186
Planting Chart 20
Plums
Fruity Yogurt Pots 162
Pomegranate Seeds
Pink Dip 98
Pork
Campfire Skewers 161
Pork and Apple Burgers 158
Sausage and Veggie Sleepover 108
Pork and Apple Burgers 158
Potatoes
Campfire Skewers 161
Cheesy Root Veg Bake 111
Hedgehog Potatoes 107
How to grow 41
Sack of Potatoes 40
Sausage and Veggie Sleepover 108
Ten Veg Soup 140
Veggie Fries 96
Pots, recycled, biodegradable 14, 15, 16
Little Pots of Sunshine 181

Prawns
Rainbow Rolls 124
Present From the Garden 191
Pumpkins
How to grow 50
Orange Dip 100
Pumpkin and Courgette Fritters 145
Sausage and Veggie Sleepover 108
Squash in a Tub 49
Pumpkin and Courgette Fritters 145
Radishes
Beets the Washing Up 62
How to grow 64
Rainbow Rolls 124
Rainbow Rolls 124
Raspberries
Eton Mess Ice Cream Cake 173
Magical Chocolate Fudge Cake 153
Mint and Raspberry Lemonade 123
Ten Minute Jam 165
Recycling 14, 15, 16
Reduce Waste 16
Rhubarb
Fruity Yogurt Pots 162
Messy Tart 174
Rocket
Pesto Pasta Salad 138
Terrific Tray Bake Pizza 146
Root Vegetables
Beets the Washing Up 62
Bucket and Spade Veggies 24
Crunchy, Fruity Slaw 102
Cheesy Root Veg Bake 111
Gardener's Cake 112
Hedgehog Potatoes 107
Italian Soup 140
Ketchup 150
Magical Chocolate Fudge Cake 153
Mini but Mighty Baked Veggie Bites 104
Orange Dip 100
Pink Dip 98
Sausage and Veggie Sleepover 108
Ten Veg Soup 140
Veggie Fries 96
Rosemary
A Present From the Garden 191
Cheese and Rosemary Shortbreads 129
How to grow 30
Sausage and Veggie Sleepover 108
Shopping for Herbs 28
Runner Beans
How to Build a Tee 'Pea' 53
How to grow 54
Sack of Potatoes 40
Sage
A Present From the Garden 191
Cheese and Rosemary Shortbreads 129
How to grow 30
Pork and Apple Burgers 158
Shopping for Herbs 28
Salad Leaves
Easy-Peasy Garden Salad 119
How to grow 46

Pic 'n' Mix Lettuce 44
Rainbow Rolls 124
Squeaky Salad 120
Winter Lettuce 47
Salads
Crunchy, Fruity Slaw 102
Easy-Peasy Garden Salad 119
Pesto Pasta Salad 138
Squeaky Salad 120
Salmon
Sticky Salmon 134
Sandwiches
Snail Sandwiches 154
Sausage and Veggie Sleepover 108
Sausages
Campfire Skewers 161
Sausage and Veggie Sleepover 108
Save the Planet 16
Seasonal
Planting chart 20
Buying 16
Secateurs 10
Seed Feeders, Bird 182
Seed Library 196
Shopping for Herbs 28
Shortbread
Cheese and Rosemary 129
Flower Petal 128
Skewers
Campfire Skewers 161
Slugs 15, 57, 82
Slug Pellets
Natural 16
Smelly Feet 85
Snail Sandwiches 154
Snails, Pizza 149
Soil 10, 12
For types, see compost
Soup
Squiggly Noodle Soup 137
Ten Veg Soup 140
Sowing Chart 20
Soya Beans
Green Dip 101
Spinach
Eat Your Greens! 75
How to grow 76
Pesto Pasta Salad 138
Ten Veg Soup 140
Spray Bottle 10
Spring Onions
Green Dip 101
Plant Your Own Packed Lunch 186
Pumpkin and Courgette Fritters 145
Squiggly Noodle Soup 137
Spring Rolls
Rainbow Rolls 124
Squash in a Tub 49
Squeaky Salad 120
Squiggly Noodle Soup 137
Stem Fruits
Messy Tart 174
Sticks

Cinnamon 185
Hazel/birch 53-54
Hollow 195
Sticky Salmon 134
Stinging Nettles
How to Make Nitrogen Feed 64
Stone Fruits
Fruity Yogurt Pots 162
Messy Tart 174
Strawberries
Campfire Skewers 161
Eton Mess Ice Cream Cake 173
Host a Butterfly Banquet 192
How to grow 58
Messy Tart 174
Mint and Raspberry Lemonade 123
Strawberry Butterfly Cakes 169
Strawberry Clouds 57
Strawberry Butterfly Cakes 169
Strawberry Clouds 57
Successional Sowing 44
Summer Berries
Apple and Berry Crunch 167
Blueberry Flowerpot Muffins 170
Campfire Skewers 161
Eton Mess Ice Cream Cake 173
Fruity Yogurt Pots 162
Magical Chocolate Fudge Cake 153
Messy Tart 174
Mint and Raspberry Lemonade 123
Strawberry Butterfly Cakes 169
Ten Minute Jam 165
Sunflowers
Little Pots of Sunshine 181
Sunflower Seeds 69
Sweetcorn
Campfire Skewers 161
Rainbow Rolls 124
Sweet Potato
Veggie Fries 96
Sweetie Peas 67
Tart
Messy Tart 174
Tayberries
Apple and Berry Crunch 167
Ten Minute Jam 165
Ten Veg Soup 140
Terrific Tray Bake Pizza 146
Thinning Out 26
Thyme
A Present From the Garden 191
How to grow 30
Shopping for Herbs 28
Tomatoes
A Can of Tomatoes 37
Campfire Skewers 161
How to grow 38
Ketchup 150
Pesto Pasta Salad 138
Plant Your Own Packed Lunch 186
Rainbow Rolls 124
Sausage and Veggie Sleepover 108
Ten Veg Soup 140

Terrific Tray Bake Pizza 146
Tray Baked Pizza 146
Tree(s) 16, 34, 57, 182, 186
Broccoli Trees with Garlic Crumbs 132
Trowel 10
Trug, DIY 14, 49, 53
Vegetables
See individual
Veggie Bites 104
Veggie Fries 96
Washing Up Bowl 62
Water Sprayer, DIY 15
Watering Can, Make a 15
Welcome Wildlife 18
Wellington Boots 85, 87
We've Sprung a Leek 32
What Plants Need 10
Wildlife
Bug Hotel 195
Butterfly Banquet 192
Feed the Birds 182
Welcome 18
Window Box 70, 72, 192
Winter Lettuce 47
Worms 13
A Café for Worms 189
Year of Sowing, Planting & Harvesting 20
Yogurt
Crunchy, Fruity Slaw 102
Fruity Yogurt Pots 162
Pink Dip 98
Terrific Tray Bake Pizza 146
Yogurt Pots 14, 34, 182
Fruity Yogurt Pots 162

ACKNOWLEDGEMENTS

Julia and Ghillie would like to thank... SO many people! Below is a list of those that have made our book the corker that it is, as well as giving us the encouragement, tea and gin required to trust ourselves to bring The Little Grower's Cookbook to life.

Firstly our incredible team – Ali Allen for her beautiful photographs and patience with two enthusiastic/annoying authors! Mark Coltart for his design direction and stunning cover. Fiona Ritson for being a design and illusatration whizz as well as so patient, supportive and flexible enough to drop everything and turn this book around! The lovely Gemma, a true pro and a subbing queen. Hannah for giving us the encouragement and support to get the Little Growers up and running and lastly Annie and Elaine at TWP for their expertise.

For the photo shoot – we thank our excellent models, William, Jemima, George, Scarlett, Margot and Wilf (and the lovely and supportive Emma St John, for introducing to us her gorgeous nieces). A huge thank you also to Julia's neighbour and friend Lionel for allowing us to hop over the garden wall to use his shed for our front cover. Imogen Tyler for her styling knowledge, props and general wonder-woman assistance in the kitchen.

Amy Cameron for her expertise in digging for worms and being a great hand model and Emma Myrtle for kindly seeking out a suitable colander! Emily Tier at Cumnor House Nursery for donating redundant welly boots. Peter and Clare Evelyn for allowing Ghillie to borrow their house and kitchen, Ness and Ella for the best kids staycation and Simon for giving Ghillie the courage to ask the legend that is Olivia Colman if she liked our book enough to write a forward for it. Thanks Olivia, you made our year!

Jess and Simon Webb, Thomas Neve, Sophie A, Jess D, Frog and Mark Keenan for their much needed advice about the world of publishing and to John Vincent and Lucinda Miller for saying such lovely things about our book. To Caroline Bishop for her insight into forest schools and sustainable projects. To Sam Rice, Alicia Walker, Pippa G, Lindsay B, Antonia F, Wheezie, Tula, Shona, Helen and Andrew Gilliespie-Smith and so many others (you know who you are) for being such great sounding boards.

Our families for unwavering support throughout the entire process, but especially before, during and after the photo shoot (notably Nick who even did the washing up!). You have been rockstars the lot of you!

Lastly, a big thank you to our parents for giving us both the safe and extremely happy childhoods that have inspired us enough to want to write this book.

More thank you's to all the many kind folk who have donated, lent props and tested recipes:

Burgon & Ball, adult and children's garden tools burgonandball.com
Doodie Stark, women's clothing doodiestark.co.uk
Marshalls Seeds UK marshalls-seeds.co.uk
Molly Mahon, fabrics and homewares mollymahon.com
Nutscene Twine nutscene.com
Olivier Baby, children's clothing olivierbaby.com
Pushpanjali, linens and enamelware pushpanjalitrading.com
The Linen Works, clothing and linens thelinenworks.co.uk
Thompson & Morgan UK, garden supplies thompson-morgan.com

Livs Bradshaw
Fiona and Grace Cameron
Kirsty Cornell
Jane Drysdale
Clare and Gina Evelyn
Kate Hannah
Hilary James
Boo and Rory J-D
Gardie J-D
Tania MacCallum
Soph Martin
Lou Medhurst
Nomi Miller
Helen Paguntalan
Karen Pilkington
Alice Smith
Ed and Nicola Stockreisser
Becca Taylor